QUEST FOR FREEDOM:
THE SCOTS-IRISH PRESBYTERIAN REBELLIONS FOR POLITICAL AND RELIGIOUS FREEDOM

WILLIAM MOORE and DAVID B. NOLAN

6-15-17

To Mike

From. Peggy

DEDICATION

The authors dedicate this book to Scotland's Presbyterian Covenanters and freedom fighters for religious and political liberty. These include: Patrick Simson and his grandsons George and Patrick Gillespie, who are Scottish ancestors of co-author William E. Moore. The authors recognize North Carolina minister David Caldwell, who preached heroically against the British abuses, and William Moore's colonial American ancestors Congressman James Gillespie, an influential U. S. Congressman, and pioneer surveyor son David. Congressman Gillespie and son, David, were descendants of George Gillespie, Westminster Assemblies renowned theologian. These freedom fighters challenged the English Crown's authoritarian rule as to forced Anglicanism and political subjugation.

Presbyterians served as ministers, soldiers and legislators, to support steadfastly Scotland and America's "Quest for Freedom". Their Calvinistic religious and political philosophy was coupled with a courageous will to fight for the right of common man. They supported the Puritan Reformation, and Glorious Revolution in the British Isles. They dominated America's Revolutionary War to overturn the English monarchy's Kingly Right's Rule, also known as the "Divine Right of Kings".

NOTES FOR READERS

Humble Scots-Irish worshipers carried their quest for religious and political freedom from England to Ulster to Colonial America. Their deeply engrained populist government ideals ensured America's individual liberty for the common man.

(The authors researched Scots-Irish lore and historical information in the public domain for this book. Special thanks go to the Wikipedia Foundation and its founder, Jimmy Walls, for identifying reliable source documentation.) The authors make no claim as to the total accuracy of these astonishing Scots-Irish stories.

ACKNOWLEDGEMENT

The Scots-Irish Presbyterians fought to ensure their religious and political beliefs would prevail over royal authoritarian attempts to impose universal Catholicism, and later universal Anglicanism. They led the Protestant Reformation and the Glorious Revolution that put a Protestant on the English throne in 1688. They crusaded for "liberty of conscience". These determined Scots-Irishmen sailed to America seeking freedom and were instrumental in colonial America's winning freedom of religious choice, and political independence from the English Crown.

The Gillespie family over generations with their motto, Esse quam videri (to be rather than to seem), supported fully the Scots-Irish resolve for religious and political liberty. They led the Presbyterian Reformation over the dictatorial reign of the Stuart Kings in England.

The Gillespie family history has been handed down from one generation to another by oral tradition and kept correspondence. It chronicles their contributions to this movement and American culture today.

We thank everyone who provided their creative guidance, priceless anecdotes, and their enthusiasm for memorializing this freedom movement from Scotland, to Ulster, and then to colonial America. We specially recognize for assistance Beverly Tetterton of the New Hanover County Public Library, Wilmington, North Carolina. Dr. Richard Schrader former head Librarian of University of North Carolina's Southern Historical Library and Dr. Dallas Herring, former Chairman of North Carolina's State Board of Education.

We also thank the dedicated staff of the Library of Congress, National Archives, University of North Carolina's Southern Historical Library, North Carolina's State Archives, and Scotland's University of Glasgow and their assistance in locating key historical documents.

We recognize authors Gary Amos and Richard Gardiner for their book, "Never Before in History", which memorializes the theological leadership of Martin Luther, John Calvin, and John Knox, who each influenced America's freedom from the Anglican Church orthodoxy. Amos and Gardiner, so masterfully, describe how the ever-determined Puritans transformed their steadfast beliefs for **"liberty of conscience"**, especially religious liberty, into freedom from the Crown in the new American nation. The "Westminster Confession", which George Gillespie co-drafted, was the most widely published and read text, second only to the Bible, in Colonial America.

Colonial Presbyterians insisted that an amendment be included in the Constitution that guaranteed religious freedom as part of their legacy.

The authors also thank Senator Jim Webb of Virginia with his enthusiastic book, "Born Fighting", for modern day inspiration in the freedom fighter tradition. His observations chronicle the Scots-Irish cultural contributions for rugged individualism, distrust of centralized authority, and loyalty to leadership that follows principle.

The English Crown and Anglican aristocracy repressed the rights of common man on both sides of the Atlantic. Upon arrival in America, the Gillespies, like most other Scots-Irish Presbyterians, recoiled from their unfair-horrific experiences in the British Isles. Their intense antipathy towards abuse of power by the English Crown led to revolutionary fervor in America.

As described by Webb, these born-fighting Scots-Irish had little tolerance for further abuse of royal power in the American Colonies. They had enormous sympathy for the plight of the common man. Webb confirmed that the Scots-Irish plea for "common man rights" fashioned America's freedom spirit and democratic traditions. America's populist Government ideals and principles are reflected in the ascendancy of Andrew Jackson as the first

U. S. President of Scots-Irish heritage

The authors thank the American Sovereignty Task Force, a 501(c) (3) organization, and the Federal Ethics Center for insights into the origins of the "Bill of Rights" to the U. S. Constitution.

CONTENTS

INTRODUCTION

The authors seek an entertaining presentation of the successful struggle of Scots-Irish Presbyterians for religious and political liberty. The Gillespie family's common vision over centuries of God's given right of freedom from authoritarian abuses merely mirrors that of their fellow Scots-Irish. History should not only be limited to tales of the political expediency of monarchs. Achievements that changed the world were made by the heroics of the common man who overcame adversity.

This astonishing story of the Presbyterian rebellions in their fight for political and religious freedom chronicles the Gillespie family and their fellow, Scots-Irish, Presbyterians in their freedom battles from William Wallace to the American Revolutionaries. These humble worshipers curbed successfully the exclusive power of English Kings. The establishment of the U.S. Constitution and Bill of Rights is their legacy to limited federal government today.

Through the ages, the religious rights of these ever-determined Scottish Presbyterians were continuously violated by the menacing "Kingly Rights" under the pretext that God had approved such royal fiat over subjects. The common man's freedom over the centuries ebbed and flowed depending on each particular English monarch's necessity for compromise to remain in power.

The emphasis of the Presbyterians in the express "Word of God" and their influence by Calvinistic doctrine of predestination drove their necessity for religious freedom. Their philosophy was expressed by Scotland's renowned theologians including John Knox, John Milton, Samuel Rutherford, George Gillespie, and John Locke. Each Presbyter provided a steadfast avenue to express religious zeal within their respective kirks.

Struggling over many years, these Scots, mostly Presbyterian, expressed their populist governing ideals.

They carried their idealistic thinking from Scotland, across the North Channel to Ulster, and finally across the Atlantic to America compelling America's new democracy.

Unwilling to yield in their religious beliefs and democratic ideals these Puritans suffered from the cruelties and corruptions of the English Crown. Described is their freedom crusade and religious reformation in Scotland, and their historic battles in Ireland, supporting King William's Glorious Revolution of 1688 against the oppression of King James II and his Catholic supporters.

During the murderous times of the Stuart Kings, the English Puritans struggled desperately to end the authoritarianism of Charles II, the cruelty of his brother James Duke of York, and the greed of their bishop operatives. One such effort to rid England of the Stuart control was the "Rye House Plot", an assassination plot staged from the fortified Rye House mansion. Suspected of being involved in an assassination conspiracy, John Locke and many other Puritans fled for their lives to the Netherlands to escape the wrath of James. In the Netherlands, Locke continued to write and document his religious and political philosophy.

Locke's political theme that "man has the right to defend life, liberty and pursuit of happiness" impressed Thomas Jefferson. This theme later influenced Jefferson's drafting of the Declaration of Independence and America's completion of the U.S. Constitution and Bill of Rights.

The zeal of the Covenanters overcame the intransigence of the Stuart Kings. A number of distinguished Presbyterian ministers, within the Gillespie-Simson family, preached openly against the Crown's self-serving doctrine of Kingly Rights. The descendants of George Gillespie, the leader of the Westminster Assembly, carried this philosophical fervor to colonial Carolina.

The Presbyterians led America's campaign for religious freedom from the Church of England controlled by the Crown. They led the fight to establish the First Amendment to *the U. S. Constitution* and to ensure freedom of worship across the Atlantic.

British General Cornwallis and Loyalists to the Crown labeled the revolution for American Independence a "Presbyterian Rebellion" which caused the English King to lose the American Colonies. Presbyterian clergy and their congregations were so feared as adversaries that British forces burned seventy (70) of their houses of worship in the colonies so as to prevent further political dissent against the Crown.

Approximately one-third of all colonists were active Tories who supported the Crown in attempting to crush the American Revolution. In contrast, Presbyterian congregations of the small farmer and common man strongly supported the American Revolution to establish democracy and ensure individual liberty.

Many Scots-Irish revolutionaries suffered severe repercussions for challenging the royal power. Future U. S. President, Andrew Jackson, was slashed in the face as a teenager for refusing to polish the boots of a British soldier. His older brother, Robert, died of his wounds in a British Army prison for his political opposition to the English Crown. British forces also burned the homes of Presbyterian leaders of the American Revolution including the home of James Gillespie from the Village of Grove, near Wilmington, North Carolina. This hero of America's religious and political freedom serving in North Carolina's Senate ensured that America's Constitutional government had provisions for the common man including the Bill of Rights. James Gillespie prevailed to serve in early sessions in the U. S. Congress as an Anti-Federalist continually fighting for the rights of common man as his Scottish ancestors had over centuries. Congressman James Gillespie's ancestors in Scotland and fellow freedom fighters carried their struggle for religious and political liberty to North America.

The roots of U. S. Constitutional government and individual rights must be understood to prevent their infringement. All Americans should fully appreciate the enormous contributions and sacrifices these brave, born-fighting, determined Scots Irishmen, typically Presbyterian from Ulster, provided during the Revolutionary War. Their unyielding struggles for political and religious freedom had a significant impact on the founding of America. These ever-determined Presbyterians and all Americans were finally free from the Crown's unjust tyrannical rule.

Through this story of the Presbyterian rebellions for political and religious freedom, the authors strive to provide everyone; especially the citizens of America and the United Kingdom, a better understanding and appreciation of these brave, heroic, Scots-Irish Presbyterians and their unwaveringly pursuit of freedom.

The Puritan's freedom crusade essentially began when Luther, in 1517, nailed his 95 theses on the Wittenberg Church door. Luther determinedly sat forth his belief for "liberty of conscience", which rang Puritan philosophy throughout the following centuries, "people should be free to believe whatever religious faith they hold true; both government and church must allow for their religious freedom."

PART I- Scotland's Yearning for Freedom (1296-1603)

"We as Scots, fight not for glory, nor riches, nor honour, but for our FREEDOM!"
-William Wallace

Statue of William Wallace- Scotland's Fierce Warrior in Aberdeen, Scotland

The Scots' independence had roots to their ancient Pict ancestors who fought successfully against the Romans. The Romans with their highly trained, well equipped, Army had conquered England.

These Picts' pluck and their endurance in the 2nd century A.D encouraged absolute loyalty within their tribes from the bottom up; i.e. from warriors to their clan chieftain. This brotherhood loyalty of the early Scots to the freedom cause continued to 14th century battles led by Scottish leader William Wallace against English King

Edward I. The Scottish fight against subjugation continued with Scottish King Robert the Bruce against English King Edward II.

The heroic, brave struggles of Scotland's freedom warriors, led by Wallace and Bruce, gained Scotland's independence under their Aberoth Treaty, which declared Scotland an independent nation.

With the oncoming of Bloody Mary's murderous reign to restore the Catholic Church to power in England, many brave Puritans fled Scotland to Geneva where they joined Calvin's Protestant campaign. Calvin's "Institutes of Christian Religion" inspired the Presbyterian religion and political reformation of the 16th and later centuries. The Puritan philosophy shaped many of our founding fathers' political views in their drive for religious freedom and Democracy in America.

Having endured centuries of religious manipulation and denial of rule law under the Papist influenced Crown brave Scottish Puritans yearned for religious freedom. They were inspired by John Knox who began Scotland's 16th century religious reformation crusade.

The reign of Queen Elizabeth I cast off Catholic control as had that of her father Henry VIII. She supported Cranmer's "Book of Common Prayer" which revived Puritan theology in England.

Like other European countries, Scotland over the ages had endured the many Catholic Church corruptions greatly influenced by and largely controlled by the Pope, and enforced by the monarchs. The Scots continually faced the Crown's many horrific cruelties; thus, they had an enormous yearning for religious freedom. Driven by their hunger for freedom from these corruptions, Scotland's devoted theologians began their religious reformation. Reverend Knox, with his undying Calvinistic beliefs, led the Presbyterian reformation. Upon the death of Knox, Patrick Simson and his son-in-law John Gillespie, minister of Kirkcaldy's historic Kirk, joined the Melvilles, Dicksons, Bruces, and other unwavering theologians to drive Scotland's religious freedom crusade into the 17th century.

Chapter 1
Scotland's Early Freedom Struggles

"**FREEDOM!! FREEDOM!!**" William Wallace screamed as he was hanged before his neck was broken. King Edward's tortures continued as Wallace was disemboweled to end his, brave, freedom-loving life. Edward then ordered Wallace's body to be drawn and quartered by four horses. Edward gruesomely beheaded the brave warrior. As a warning to all Scottish warriors, Edward hideously spiked Wallace's tarred skull on London Bridge for all crossing the Thames River to view.

Wallace firmly believed, "**FREEDOM** is the best of all things and that God gave us life jointly with **LIBERTY.**" This Scottish warrior declared: "We fight not for glory, honour, nor riches; but for our **FREEDOM.**"

Following the murder of Wallace, and after nearly five centuries, the Scots continued to fight subjugation by the English Crown. America's Scots- Irish immigrants reflected the brave born-fighting spirit of their Scottish ancestors. Patrick Henry and other Scots-Irish were the catalysts for victory over England in each colony.

The Authors "Quest for Freedom" story begins in 1296 when:

> - England's King Edward I's huge army seized and destroyed the city of Berwick and brutally killed over 17,000 Scots. Edward burned most of the surrounding hamlets. He anticipated that his terrorism would create fear throughout Scotland and facilitate subjugation.

However, Edward I underestimated the fierce and determined will of these Scots. The barbaric burning of seventy (70) Presbyterian Churches in the Colonies did not deter the Scots-Irish Presbyterians' fighting will in a seven year war for independence from King George III.

Despite superior weaponry and warfare tactics of Roman legions, these Scots maintained independence from the Roman Empire. These fearsome Picts even forced Emperor Hadrian in 125 A.D. to build his famous fortification, a wall 73 miles long and 14 feet high, across Scotland, from the Atlantic Ocean to the North Sea.

King Edward could not have been more mistaken in thinking he could crush the Scottish spirit. Instead, his atrocities created a blazing fire in the spirit of these freedom loving Scottish warriors. Led by William Wallace, Scotland's brave warriors attacked fiercely with uncompromising vengeance across Scotland. They destroyed the City of York in the North of England.

Wallace was enraged when a malicious English Knight cowardly murdered his elderly father. In revenge, Wallace with his trusted band of rebels viciously attacked the many English Knights from the dense foliage of the Ettrick Forest. They terrorized King Edward in his efforts to control the determined Scots.

Thousands of Scots patriotically joined commoner Wallace against King Edward who was known as the "Hammer." Wallace used guerilla-fighting tactics throughout the Scottish countryside against the invading English attackers. Fighting triumphantly, Wallace soon recaptured much of the Scottish countryside, including the town of Scone. Wallace and his fierce fighters overwhelmed Edward's mighty army at Stirling Bridge. Following Wallace's heroic victory, Edward furiously announced all through his Kingdom, "This outlaw, Scottish thug, Wallace must be captured!"

To protect their estates from the wrath of Edward, several powerful Scottish Lords secretly divulged the location of Wallace's band of warriors to Edward. Edward's powerful army trapped Wallace and his brave followers at Falkirk. To ensure his victory, Edward hideously ordered his deadly long bow, Welsh, archers to shower arrows down on both Army's soldiers killing both English and Scots a-like. The battle continued until King Edward's army annihilated Wallace's warriors.

For five long years Wallace avoided capture. Sadly, in 1301, a compatriot betrayed Wallace and allowed Edward's soldiers to capture Wallace near Edinburgh. In mockery, the Crown's rogues tied Wallace to a pole and paraded him through the Scottish and English countryside. In London King Edward's royal court held a mock court at Westminster Abby and convicted Wallace of treason.

Following King Edward's murder of Wallace, Robert Bruce, much encouraged by Wallace's sheer determination and bravery, continued Scotland's fight for independence. In 1306, Bruce gained the Scottish throne by killing his chief rival, John Comyn ,during their private meeting in Dumfries Church. In order to avoid prosecution Bruce declared himself the Scottish King.

Internecine fighting among Scotland's war lords was common and toughened the Scottish people as warriors. Scotland's cold and wet winters were harsh and promoted hardiness as a people.

In 1314, Bruce, against all superior odds, defeated King Edward II and his English army at Bannockburn. Edward II marched his army of 20,000 royalists into Scotland to recapture the Scottish highlands. Bruce, greatly outnumbered by Edward's huge army, shrewdly chose his pre-chosen battleground with unexpected obstacles. Bruce dug many trenches that were carefully camouflaged with brush. The fine steeds of the English knights stumbled in these traps when they galloped into battle. Bruce's battlefield strategy was to force the advancing English army into a narrow area between the Firth of Forth River and the river's marsh.

Prior to battle, Bruce rode out in front of his army.

In shining armor, one of Edward's knights with his lance galloped toward Bruce. The knight charged viciously at Bruce who was armed only with his battle-axe and no armor. Bruce, using expert horsemanship, spun alongside the English Knight as he charged past on his fine mount. Bruce viciously swung his axe and crushed the knight's skull. After breaking the handle of his battle-axe, Bruce grumbled, "My axe handle is surely worth more than one English rogue's skull". Bruce's expert horsemanship and valiant performance awed nearby soldiers from both armies.

Using cunning military strategy, Bruce, like a fox trapping its prey, lured Edward's army into a narrow strip of land for battle. Edward did not realize the extent of his Army's dilemma. Bruce had drawn the English into his trap. The English Army, boxed by swamp bogs on both sides, had their backs against the River Forth. Across their battlefront were the fearsome Scottish warriors with their deadly long spears.

The brave Scottish warriors charged furiously into the English forces, and with their ingenious, defensive, spear hedgerow, used earlier by Wallace, confused and terrorized King Edward's army. Prior to Edward's invasion, Bruce trained his soldiers with their long spears to form an impenetrable, defensive, hedgerow which the Scottish warriors called a schiltron. The English Cavalry frantically charged forward in an effort to break down the awesome Scottish wall of spears. Driven by the beat of their war drums, Edward's Cavalry rode headlong into the spear schiltron. The harder the English Cavalry charged the more the relentless hedgerow of Scottish spears gutted their horses. The furious battle became a roaring melee of English knights and Scottish warriors. English knights fell off their staggering wounded horses. Edward's bewildered knights, entangled with their stumbling steeds, fought furiously against the enraged Scottish warriors. Darkness submerged the battlefield and the day's battle ended in a bloody combat.

Under the cover of darkness, both Armies retreated to plan their battle strategy for the next day. King Edward's army bottled up in the muddy swamp along the Firth of Forth found little dry ground for a night's rest.

As dawn approached, Bruce cleverly changed his military strategy to the offensive. Bruce's offensive maneuver surprised the English as his brave warriors charged fiercely with their long and sharp spears directly into the English troops. The Scots had shrewdly boxed the English into a narrow battlefield with marsh on both sides, and the Firth of Forth River at high tide, in their rear. Seizing their military advantage, the Scottish warriors fiercely attacked across the battlefront and forced chaos among the English knights.

Bruce heroically, with his army's drums beating, commanded his Scottish warriors, "**Charge--- Charge**", as the Scottish forces struck. This day's battle raged into a hand-to-hand fight to the death.

Unlike the battle of Falkirk in which feared expert Welsh archers with their longbows devastated Wallace, the English refused to shoot their rain of arrows onto the charging Scottish warriors. They feared their arrows would hit their fellow Englishmen.

Bruce gained an enormous victory at Bannockburn. The brave Scots chased Edward's Army as they staggered across the Scottish highlands, southward, back to London. The Scottish troops captured King Edward's huge wagon train of supplies and gold as the English frantically fled. King Edward, if he were victorious, had planned to enjoy lavish living in the Scottish countryside.

Instead of such opulence for Edward's rogues, Bruce so joyfully distributed King Edward's bounty of fineries among his faithful and well-deserving, servants and warriors.

Bruce's victory at Bannockburn led to a truce with the English. In 1320, England acknowledged to Scotland the Aberoth Declaration of Independence. The Scots included in their independence document, "We as Scots, fight not for glory, nor riches, nor honour; but for our **"FREEDOM."**

Their Arberoth instilled for the Scots an ongoing expectation of freedom. These Scots brought their desire for freedom to the American colonies. American founding fathers of Scots-Irish lineage included most signers of the Declaration of Independence.

Thomas Jefferson was greatly stirred by Scotland's Arberoth. During Jefferson's schooling at the College of William and Mary, Scottish Professor William Small introduced the future president to the writings of Scottish Lord Henry Karnes and John Locke. Jefferson drew upon their insights as to liberty of conscience when he drafted America's Declaration of Independence from the British Empire.

The bravery of Wallace and Bruce in the first decade of the 14th century and the Picts' spirit against the Roman Empire was continued by Scotland's Presbyterians. Several centuries after the successes of Wallace and Bruce, the Presbyterians continued their flame for "FREEDOM" in their religious reformation struggles against the Stuart monarchs. Upon emigrating to America, these determined zealots for freedom gained independence for the American colonies from England.

Bruce's heroic victory at Bannockburn resolved two vital national issues for Scotland. The English recognized Scotland as a nation and Catholic Pope John XXII issued a proclamation that the King of Scotland would be henceforth recognized as a national sovereign by the Catholic Church.

After the death of Bruce, the English in later centuries continued to seek the control of Scotland, and over the 15th and 16th century they continually attacked Scotland. Among England's many murderous attacks were the destruction of Berwick and fiery attacks of Flodden and Solway Mass. These onslaughts were followed by King Henry's "Rough Wooing" campaign of terror over Scotland.

Cleverly, King Henry VIII in his grand scheme to dominate Scotland negotiated the Treaty of Greenwich. Terms of the Treaty provided that his year-old son, Prince Edward, would marry Mary Queen of Guise's infant daughter Mary. Fearing for her daughter's life, Queen Mary refused for her daughter Mary to marry King Henry's son Edward. King Henry became enraged and he ordered his Earl of Hertford to annihilate the Scots.

Hertford's savage attacks on Scotland are famously remembered as King Henry's "Rough Wooing". Commander Hertford ordered every man, woman, and child be put to fire and sword and that Edinburgh be burned. King Henry declared, "We bring the vengeance of God upon Scotland for their disloyalty and falsehood." Henry's hideous attacks resulted in the destruction of many Scottish towns, including Edinburgh and Dunbar.

Not only did Scotland have to contend with the English Crown's constant attacks of the 15th and 16th centuries, they also contended with unending rampant inter clan violence and the acts of reckless, ineffective, Scottish monarchs.

During England's continual attacks on Scotland, the Scots were devastated by the "Black Death", bubonic plague, spread by flea bites, and the rampant spread of deadly Smallpox. These extremely deadly diseases wiped out over 20% of Scotland's population.

By the early 1500's, the Catholic Church throughout Europe became unduly authoritarian to gain financially from indulgences. Over the 15th and 16th centuries, the Church transitioned from religion to a self-serving commercial business focused on control of the masses. Pope Julius II ignored the many atrocious corruptions throughout England. Rome was in league with England's ruling class that furthered the financial interests of the universal Church.

The ongoing failure of the Catholic Church to cleanse itself under the sponsorship of the Pope was enabled by intransigent cardinals, bishops, and priests who desired to maintain the *status quo* of order. Other European monarchs remained silent since they also wanted continuation of the partnership for centralized control.

Such corrupting influences were self-perpetuating and orchestrated by abuse of power. The Church's failures included:

(1) The Pope controlling, according to his whim, the appointment of bishops, priors, deans, cardinals, monks and priests.

(2) Indulgences-Catholic cardinals, bishops and priests furthered Catholic construction of Cathedrals through the "forgiveness" of parishioner sins by priests exploiting guilt over sins. There were certain sins, supposedly, only the Church official on behalf of God could pardon. When such a sin occurred the official received, in many cases, huge sums for the absolution.

(3) Appointment of church officials that were relatives or friends of a papal leader. In many cases they were ill equipped to serve God or parishioners. Lifetime pensions were provided for corrupt friends of the Church.

(4) Catholic positions were sold for huge profits and were shared throughout monasteries and within the ranks of the ruling class.

A favorite "jingle" during these corrupt times that vividly depicted the Puritans' disgust over the indulgency corruptions of the Catholic Church is:

"When the coin in the coffer rings,
A soul from purgatory springs!"

So unbelievably gluttonous, Pope Leo X in 1517 began a fund drive to sell indulgences all across Europe, particularly in Germany, to pay for an extensive renovation of St Peter's Basilica in Rome. This furthered the Pope's taste of fine art, including Michelangelo's celebrated murals in Rome. The Pope during this period appointed a number of Archbishops in return for debt relief. Using the Archbishop's debts, the Pope imposed schemes (sale of indulgences and clerical positions) to raise immense funds to renovate St Peter's Basilica.

In Wittenberg Germany Martin Luther objected to the Vatican's divergences from Christian doctrine. Luther and fellow worshipers became infuriated by Papal intransigence towards reform.

In a rage, Luther wrote his "Ninety Five Theses" that described Puritan objections to the rampant corruptions throughout the hierarchy of the Catholic Church. Martin Luther used "All Saints Day" to time his objections and nailed his famous "Ninety Five Theses" to the door of Wittenberg's Castle Church. Luther's concerns were the primary catalyst that ignited the Protestant Reformation in Europe.

The robust minded Scots, from Earls and Lords down to the lowest villager, detested the Catholic Church's aberrations from traditional Christianity from the time of Pope Peter.

The Catholic Church exerted great control over the lives of Europeans to the West of the realm of the Greek Orthodox Church. Along with royal and parliamentary laws, township and guild rules, Catholic Church dictates controlled most European lives. The Pope controlled the Catholic Realm and, therein, he could and did control laws of the land, mint money, grant land holdings, and approve the marriages of the monarchs. The Pope anointed the heads of many European countries and proclaimed that their authority was an integral part of God's plan.

Therefore, Europe's rulers hesitated to criticize or attack the institution that had validated their rule as God's divine right.

In 1532 another example of the many corruptions of the Catholic Church was Scotland's King James V's urging of Pope Clement VII to appoint his three illegitimate sons as Abbots and Priors. His bastards received a handsome income at the expense of Scottish parishioners who were compelled to donate to the Catholic Church.

Scotland's King James V was allied to France and Catholicism. He was so closely tied with Pope Clement that the Pope allowed James to tax the income of monasteries to fill his Royal coffer. When Henry VIII of England broke ties with the Pope and Catholicism, he tried on several occasions without success to convince King James of Scotland to sever ties with Rome. Scotland especially welcomed the Protestant Reformation that was long overdue.

During the year 1560 in England on the eve of Scotland's reformation, the Catholic Church raked in over 300,000 pounds in English currency. At this time, the Catholic Church had amassed more than a third of the English land and half of the country's wealth.

Scotland's many long years of harsh struggles against Catholic Church excesses, coupled with their fervor to establish their Presbyterian faith, created a burning desire throughout the Scottish countryside for freedom of religion and individual liberties.

Over 200,000 Scots-Irish migrated to Colonial America by the mid- 18th century. They brought their desire for freedom and liberty to America, along with a huge distrust of and dislike for the English Crown abuses.

Their enormous struggles against Papist support of English Kings, and aberrations from traditional Christian practices, confirmed their beliefs in establishment of Presbyters to run local churches. They held centralized religious power with suspicion and distrust.

Scotland's renowned theologians, led by John Knox, engrained Calvinistic influence among Presbyterian souls. These Scots developed a huge appreciation for individualism over autocratic centralized control.

Their fervent religious zeal, as preached within their kirks, shaped and solidified democratic philosophy of their close-knit egalitarian clan society. They believed and practiced that democracy is "of the people, for the people, and by the people". Their religious and political philosophy equalized the worth of the lowest villager with that of the Lords and Barons.

A century later during the reign of Charles I, Samuel Rutherford wrote his famous book, "Lex Rex" (Law is King), which personified Presbyterians' self-governing beliefs under divine providence. His writing directly challenged the top down social order of the Catholic and Anglican Church, and directly contradicted and assaulted the divine rights of Kings and royal nobility to monopolize religion and governance.

Family and community independence in religion and politics supported the Presbyterian movement for religious freedom. Their beliefs in support of common man opposed tyranny. The Presbyterian reformation insisted that the existing top down authority structure of the Catholic Church run by priests and king appointed officials, called bishops, would be replaced by local appointment within their villages. Boroughs of Presbyterian parishioners would be served by locally appointed church elders.

These elders participated in church courts to oversee community and regional affairs. Presbyterianism placed local authority at the core of church power. Local village authority supported by the Kirk became the vehicle to fight any abusive power that violated individual rights in the community. The hierarchy of the Presbyterian Church consists of the local church, the Kirk, governed by a body of elected elders called the presbytery. Under a synod are a number of Presbyteries and at the top of this structure is the country's general assembly whose officials are ministers and elders from the presbyteries.

Into the middle 16th Century the English crown continued under Mary Tudor to force Catholic liturgy upon her subjects. When Mary Tudor ascended the British throne, she did her utmost to restore Catholicism throughout England and Scotland.

During her reign, English Protestants feared her as Bloody Queen Mary (1544-1555). Pope Gregory XIV ignored these horrific cruelties of compulsion. Mary's many supporters inflicted all means of punishment on the freedom-loving Protestants. A historical record of the Crown's supported cruelties, during the reign of Mary Tudor, is Fox's gruesome volume, "Book of Martyrs". Fox records the burning of Protestant worshipers at the stake. Fox describes the lives and the horrific burning of these humble and determined worshipers in their quest for religious freedom. Included in Mary's burning is Thomas Cranmer, whom Henry VIII appointed within his Anglican Church as Archbishop of Canterbury.

In contrast, Queen Elizabeth, to support her Puritan reign, selected Cranmer's famous "Book of Common Prayer" for England's ritual.

During Bloody Mary's campaign to crush Protestants, John Knox and William Whittingham fled Scotland to Geneva to escape her murderous wrath. Many Puritans safely joined John Calvin in Geneva to continue their religious beliefs.

Meanwhile, all across Europe, the Puritans especially disgusted with Catholicism vigorously sought reformation of the authoritarian Papal rule.

John Knox, a Catholic priest earlier in life, had witnessed first-hand the worsening of Catholic repression. Unable to accept the Catholic Church's growing aberrations he joined the Puritans in their crusade for religious freedom and justice.

Early in the Puritans' rebellion, the Catholics arrested Presbyterian minister George Wishart for heresy. Cardinal Beaton, who was well known for his patriotic stance against Henry VIII's Protestant beliefs, led the Papists in their attacks against the reforming Puritans and they burned Wishart at the stake. In retaliation, the Puritans murdered Cardinal Beaton and took control of the Castle at St. Andrews.

Fed up with the intransigence of the Catholic Church, John Knox, known as the rebel priest, joined the Puritans in their siege of the Castle. Finally, France, in support of Mary of Guise, attacked the Puritans and retook their St. Andrews Castle stronghold. In their assault, the French Papists captured a number of Puritans, including Knox. The French placed Knox in chains and imprisoned him on board a sailing vessel for several years as a galley slave. With a fighting spirit, like that of William Wallace and Robert Bruce, Knox escaped his bondage and joined John Calvin and William Whittingham and a number of other Puritan scholars in Geneva, Switzerland.

During their asylum in Geneva, several of the Protestant scholars, led by Whittingham, oversaw the translation of the Bible into their Geneva Puritan Bible. Whittingham and his fellow scholars labored, day and night, to draft an English translation of the Bible, which they energetically wrote with unwavering, puritanical spirit. These determined theologians ensured that there are many marginal notes to provide a better understanding of the scripture and to explain that God rather than the King is the Supreme Being.

Their insistence that God, rather than the King, is their supreme being angered the royal family and many Anglican bishops. Making good use of Johannes Gutenberg's printing press innovation, the Puritans in 1557 printed many copies of their Geneva Bible for wide distribution.

Whittingham and his Geneva associates published in a separate book the Chapter of Psalms from the Bible. They diplomatically dedicated their special Chapter of Psalms to Queen Elizabeth as she ascended the English throne. Whittingham and his colleagues expressed their appreciation for Queen Elizabeth's Puritan beliefs and prepared a flowery letter to the Queen declaring her accession to the English throne as a special blessing from God. With Elizabeth on the throne, the Geneva Puritans returned to Scotland and England to resume their religious goals.

Chapter 2

Queen Elizabeth's Puritan Reign

The many fanatical attacks of Bloody Mary, Queen Elizabeth's half- sister, to exterminate all Protestants in England ended upon her death. Fortuitously for the Protestant Reformation Elizabeth I was crowned Queen of England in 1558. With Elizabeth on the throne, John Knox returned from asylum in Geneva and resettled in Scotland with Calvin's "Geneva Book of Common Order" to provide a foundation for the Presbyterian faith. Scotland's Puritans were led by many brave theologians including the Gillespies, Simsons, Leslies, Melvilles, Bruces, and Camerons. These spirited theologians rallied around Knox to lead Scotland's Protestant Reformation. In 1560 they drafted Scotland's "Confession of Faith".

Mary Queen of Scots, from 1559 to 1560, resided in France with her husband King Francis and was absent from Scotland's return to Protestantism. Upon returning to Scotland, she hesitated to interfere with Scotland's Reformation. Mary remarked, "I fear John Knox's sermons more than a Scottish warrior's sword." Scotland's theologians met for several years to draft and ratify their "Confession of Faith", which provided guidelines for Scotland's Presbyterian Church. Knox was supported and protected by the Protestant rule of Queen Elizabeth. She enabled the establishment of Scotland's Presbyterian Church.

During her royal reign, Knox had a number of unpleasant encounters with Scotland's Queen Mary. Queen Mary and Knox clashed when he preached against her Catholic marriage to Don Carlos, son of King Philip II of Spain. Mary furiously scolded Knox, "What are ye within this Commonwealth?" Knox replied back, "A subject born within the same."Mary burst into tears as Knox sternly remarked, "I would rather endure your tears than remain silent and betray my Commonwealth."

When Mary married Henry Stuart, Protestant nobles vociferously rebelled, especially John Knox. Shortly after Mary's marriage, Knox during a sermon in his ministry at St. Giles Church brashly remarked about "ungodly rulers", which caused Henry Stuart to storm furiously from the Cathedral. Knox served as minister of St Giles in Edinburgh from 1560 until his death in 1572.

Upon Knox's death, Scotland's determined theologians vehemently continued Scotland's Puritan campaign. Among Scotland's theologians who led the Puritan campaign were brothers Archibald and Patrick Simson, Patrick Melville and his nephew Andrew, John Gillespie (son in law to Patrick Simson) and John Knox's son in law, John Welsh.

In 1558 upon the death of King Philip of Spain, Elizabeth Tudor, the second daughter of King Henry VIII, claimed the English Crown. Philip had served as king following the reign of his cruel, authoritarian, wife Bloody Queen Mary. Many Catholic Bishops, from the reign of Queen Bloody Mary and King Phillip, refused to participate in Elizabeth's coronation. Bishop Oglethorpe of Carlisle finally agreed and crowned Elizabeth. During her reign, Elizabeth I, a devout Puritan, encouraged and supported the Presbyterian Reformation throughout England and Scotland.

To support her Protestant reign Elizabeth appointed a number of trusted Protestant ministers as members of her royal court. Elizabeth needed loyal ministers to provide protection from political overthrow from Jesuits and other Catholics. Her supporters within her court included William Cecil, her chief adviser, and Francis Walsingham, her secretary and faithful spymaster. The Queen's royal court warded off continuous Catholic sponsored death threats supported by Spain and France.

Religious choice became a controversial issue early in Elizabeth's rule. Her Parliament, in 1559, restored her father King Henry VIII's "Act of Supremacy".

Earlier her sister, Bloody Mary, rescinded this pro Protestant Act of their father's. Mary's rescission of this Act had plunged England's Church back into the corruptions of the Popery. To bolster her Puritan reign, Elizabeth appointed herself the title of "Supreme Governor" for the Church of England. The Queen carefully avoided the wording "supreme head" since her Protestant faith identified Christ as head of the Church.

Elizabeth took major steps to rid England of the authoritarian cruelties which existed throughout the Catholic Church under her sister Bloody Queen Mary. Elizabeth purged the many Bishops who served during Mary and Mary's husband Philip's reign. Elizabeth prohibited Catholic worship throughout her kingdom and encouraged all of England to attend the Church of England.

Infuriated by Queen Elizabeth's refusal to accept Catholicism, Pope Pius V excommunicated Elizabeth I on April 27, 1570.

Various clandestine schemes arose in the many Catholic Courts of Europe to dethrone Elizabeth and exterminate the Puritan faith in England. Elizabeth overcame continual Catholic plots for her murder. Many of these schemes against Elizabeth were confirmed in letters confiscated from the jail cell of her cousin, Mary Queen of Scots.

The young, Puritan, Queen was forced to become a shrewd strategist as she considered her Royal court's insistence to behead Mary Queen of Scots. Elizabeth, in February of 1587, faced a very difficult decision. If she listened to her court's advice to behead Mary, Elizabeth recognized the immediate and overwhelming dangers from the many Catholics of Spain and France. Meanwhile, if she did not end the continual plots through Mary's Catholic allies, Elizabeth faced probable death. Finally, with the persistence of her royal court, and personal advice of William Cecil, Queen Elizabeth reached her awesome decision and signed Mary Stewart's death warrant for the Queen of Scot's to be beheaded.

Spain's King Phillip seized this moment of Catholic sympathy created by Elizabeth's beheading of Catholic royalty and hastily readied Spain's naval Armada to conquer England.

King Phillip's naval forces of 130 ships with 20,000 soldiers far exceeded England's military forces. Spain and its warring vessels controlled the high seas. Phillip's military commanders prepared to attack England's weaker navy. The Spaniards sailed their navy into the English Channel and the destruction of Elizabeth's Puritan reign seemed almost a certainty.

In desperation, English seamen modified their small fleet of fewer than forty warships to be sleek and fast. Wisely, they equipped their fleet with long-range, Scottish cannons.

Meanwhile, England's Admiral Drake sought to delay King Philip's onslaught and led a daring surprise assault on King Philip's Armada outside the port of Cadiz. Following the delay, Phillip's huge fleet set sail with orders to destroy England. Along the seacoast, the English held outdoor prayer meetings around huge bond fires. The English desperately prayed that somehow, someway, they could escape slaughter from the most powerful naval force in world history.

England had the advantage of faster and more maneuverable warships. After an initial stalemate, the Spaniards reorganized their fleet and planned an attack strategy to take advantage of their superior numbers of warring vessels.

Luckily, the smaller English fleet led by Sir Walter Raleigh was upwind from the Spanish Armada. The British seamen seized their moment and sailed a dozen warships, ablaze with explosives, directly into the center of the anchored Spanish fleet. The rapidly approaching ships on fire caused mass confusion with many collisions among the Spaniard's warships.

The Spaniards frantically turned their ships from the English coast to the open seas. From a safe distance, the daring English seamen blasted the fleeing Spanish ships with all the fire power they could muster from their superior long-range cannons. When the Spanish seamen fled to the North to circle the English Isles many of their ships were lost in a violent storm. Shipwrecked Spaniards were slaughtered by coastal English villagers. Elizabeth's navy had miraculously defeated King Phillip's huge Spanish Armada.

With defeat of the Spaniards, Elizabeth's Protestant reign was saved. In the absence of a Spanish threat, Elizabeth pursued founding Protestant colonies in North America. John Knox furthered Scotland's Presbyterian doctrine and Reformation and the Protestant movement grew throughout Scotland.

Elizabeth declared her country free of Roman Catholicism and reinstated Cranmer's "Book of Common Prayer" as the basis of Protestant theology. Elizabeth signed into law the "Act of Uniformity" which demanded consistency within the Anglican Church.

Many Protestants feared that Elizabeth, like her father, had merely replaced authoritarianism and excesses of the central power of Rome with those of the Church of England.

Under Queen Elizabeth's reign of forty-five years, England greatly prospered as a Protestant nation. England underwent a brief rebirth of freedom with a renaissance of art, literature, architecture and theater led by Shakespeare and other writers.

(Throughout the centuries, "Religious Freedom" for Scotland's Presbyterians is lost repeatedly. Fortunately, through the "Grace of God', and the steadfast efforts of Scotland's Presbyterian theologians, religious freedom for these humble worshipers ebbed and relentlessly flowed back like the mighty tides of the sea.)

Part II-The Crown's Kingly Rights (1567-1688)

The early struggles of the Scots against the English Crown reinforced self-sufficiency of the Scottish people and throughout Scotland the self-governing ethos of their humble worshipers was the antithesis of the centralized Anglican orthodoxy. These Presbyterians rejected the Anglican Church and its elaborate clerical vestments, papal oriented mass, and the liturgy's influence from Rome.

Like other European countries, Scotland, over the ages, had endured the many Catholic Church corruptions greatly influenced by, and largely controlled by the Pope and enforced by the monarchs. The Scots continually faced the Crown's many horrific persecutions; thus, they had an enormous yearning for religious freedom. Driven by their hunger for religious liberty, Scotland's devoted theologians began their religious reformation. Reverend Knox, with his undying Calvinistic beliefs, led the Presbyterian Reformation. Upon the death of Knox, Patrick Simson and his son- in- law John Gillespie, minister of Kirkcaldy's historic church, joined the Melvilles, Dicksons, Bruces, and other unwavering theologians to drive Scotland's religious freedom crusade into the 17th century.

During the Puritan's 16th century reformation, England and Scotland rejected the indulgences and other corrupting policies of the Catholic establishment. After removing much of the centuries old bondage to Catholicism, Scotland and England reformed their religious doctrine, and government, under new philosophies. The British political system gave the King and Parliament broad powers, called prerogatives, which were outside the control of official laws. The King had virtually absolute power and could deny his people rights per whim. The power of an elected Parliament could be manipulated by Kingly fiat in enforcement. King James established his Anglican Church and justified the powers of the Crown by the pretext of his **"Divine Kingly Rights"**. The Crown's divine rights were labeled the "Kingly Rights" of the monarch. James resolutely proclaimed, "No Bishop no King".

In support of his Anglican Church, James undermined Scotland's Presbytery with his many shrewd ecclesiastical maneuvers within Scotland's "General Assembly".

James I's son Charles, upon ascending to the Crown, aggressively continued his father's Anglicanism. Charles appointed more Anglican bishops in an expanded hierarchy. He forcefully imposed his "Book of Common Prayer". This slight further enraged all Presbyterians.

King Charles, with his corruptly imposed Anglican prayer book, ignored the grievances of his countrymen and continued his attempt to unify all of England and Scotland under his Anglican religion's control. Refusing to accept Charles' mandated liturgy, the humble Presbyterian worshipers throughout Scotland angrily rebelled. Led by their many faithful theologians, most of Scotland remonstrated against King Charles and his cronies.

Thousands of Scottish Puritans exhibited their determination for religious freedom and for several days stood in long lines to sign their sacred Covenant. To show their sincerity and determination, many signed their cherished pledge for religious freedom in their own blood demanding their religious liberty. These "God" fearing Calvinist reformers were resolute in their ongoing struggles with the Stuart Kings and as fighters for freedom they became known as the Covenanters.

Charles was enraged over England and Scotland's political and religious upheaval led by the Presbyterians. Charles' strong resistance to Presbyterianism, coupled with his imposed Anglicanism, erupted into a conflict which the Scots called the Bishop Wars.

Faced with almost certain military defeat in his Civil War battles against the English Parliament, led by Cromwell and the Scottish Kirks, Charles I in a desperate effort to gain military support from some of the Scots supported Scotland's cherished Covenant. He agreed that Scotland would have freedom of religion and independence.

Following the beheading of Charles I, Cromwell conquered England. During his rule under a protectorship, Oliver Cromwell dismantled England's absolute monarchy for a more representative form of government with Parliamentary rule. For a brief period, England's citizens, especially the common man, enjoyed freedom and liberties through Cromwell's Parliamentary rule. Even today, England does not have a formal Constitution similar to that of the United States. England and Scotland rely upon Parliamentary action and common law to deter abuse of discretion by central government fiat. The rule of law thus prevails over rule of man.

(Charles II seized the Crown after the death of Cromwell. King James II, the last of the Stuart Kings, horrifically persecuted the Covenanters during the dreadful era of his "Killing Fields.")

Chapter 3
King James VI's "Kingly Rights" Philosophy and his Desecration of the Presbyterian Church

Due to the many mysteries that surrounded the death of Mary Queen of Scot's husband, Henry Stuart (the Lord Darnley), Scotland's general assembly in 1567 forced Mary to abdicate her crown. Her son James Stuart, at thirteen months of age, became King of Scotland. Mary's abdication ended a twenty-five year struggle in Scotland for influence between the English Protestants and the French supported Catholics. Prior to Mary Queen of Scots fleeing to England, to avoid dealing with speculations about her complicity in her husband's murder, she gave birth to a baby boy, Prince James. Baby prince James was baptized in Chapel Royal on the grounds of Stirling Castle in accordance with Roman Catholic Rights.

In July 1567 Scotland's Queen Mary, under suspicion of murder, left her young son, James, in Sterling Castle and fled to England. With Mary, Queen of Scots, in England Scotland's Protestant Lords exercised control of young King James and held his coronation ceremony. In fear of Catholic interference his Coronation was conducted at the nearest protestant church, the Holy Rude. The Holy Rude is, down Stirling hill, just outside the protection of Sterling Castle. In fear that the many Catholics in the countryside would possibly kidnap the infant King, the Puritans, with John Knox presiding as minister, completed James' coronation ceremony in less than one hour.

The young King James' regents raised him within the Presbyterian faith in accordance with the Puritan beliefs of Scotland's ruling class. His regents personally assigned him four puritan scholars, including the learned theologian George Buchannan who fluently spoke six different languages. Buchannan taught young James to be a linguist. As a polyglot, James, as King, rarely needed a translator to conduct business with foreign heads of state.

James' schooling with Buchannan included the study of literature, writing, and foreign languages. James' superior education helped prepare him to assume the English Crown.

King James' scholarly writings were among the most influential of his era. Such a writing was James' Basilcon Doran, "The Kingly Gift". Using this writing he instructed his eldest son, Charles, as to his duties upon becoming King. Teaching from his writings about " Kingly Virtues and Duties" James taught young Charles how to rule in a most elevated manner.

Another student of Buchannan's, a classmate of James, was the Earl of Mar who throughout King James' reign was his friend and served in his royal court. The Earl resided at Stirling Castle as a member of James' royal household. James arranged the Earl of Mar's marriage to his cousin Mary Stuart, who upon marriage became the Countess of Mar. Ironically, the "Earl of Mar", through his association with Robert Cecil in England and meetings within Queen Elizabeth's royal court, much assisted James' ascension to the Crown following the death of Elizabeth.

James' royal court, during his residency at Stirling Castle, included the Earl of Mar, his Countess, and their charming daughter Lady Erskine.

Following James' marriage to his beloved wife Anne, he would accompany her and their two children, Henry and Elizabeth, and members of their royal court down the winding, steep, hill to the Holy Rude to hear the thundering sermons of minister Simson. Prince Henry and Princess Elizabeth were born during King James' residency at Stirling Castle.

Throughout the years of ministry at the Holy Rude, Patrick Simson preached before King James attempting, so ever diplomatically, to convince James that it was in his political interest for Scotland's Presbyterianism to flourish.

Minister Simson was minister at the Holy Rude until his death in 1617.

Patrick Simson, born in Perth, Scotland in 1556, was the son of Andrew Simson and Violet Adamson. Violet was the sister of renowned Patrick Adamson the Archbishop of St. Andrews. Patrick Simson married Elizabeth Hay and they had three sons who became ministers. Their daughter married John Gillespie, Minister of Kirkcaldy's Kirk. John Gillespie's two sons, during the reign of Charles I, became the renowned Covenanters, Patrick and George Gillespie. The many Presbyterian ministers, within the Simson and Gillespie families, provided much support, throughout the 16th and 17th century, to the Puritan reformation. The Simpson brothers, Patrick and Archibald ,who was the youngest, preached adamantly throughout Scotland against episcopacy. The Simsons, as did all other Presbyterians, had a special dislike for authoritarianism and corrupt Anglican bishops.

(Ironically, Gillespie is derived from the Scotch-Gaelic name *Gilleasbuig*, which means the bishop's servant. The Gaelic word *easbuig* is derived from the Latin word *episcopu*, which means bishop.)

Especially bright and studious, Patrick Simson was graduated from St. Andrews at age fourteen. Patrick pursued Greek so he could better translate ancient scripture and he became well known throughout Scotland as a Greek scholar. In 1590 the general assembly of Scotland honored Patrick Simson for his achievements in theology and appointed him to head the ministry of Stirling. Patrick Simson served as minister of Stirling, preaching at the Holy Rude (Holy Cross) from 1590 until his death in March 1618. Stirling Castle, the royal residence of King James was up a winding path and steep hill from the Holy Rude.

(Patrick Simson was Minister to The Holy Rude for 28 Years)

(Other famous Presbyterian ministers of the Holy Rude Parish, over the years, included James Guthrie. Minister Guthrie became an ardent Covenanter during Scotland's Presbyterian Revolution. He favored the Presbyterian movement over the later Anglicanism of the Stuart Kings. Guthrie served at the Holy Rude, in the 1650s, during the regency of Oliver Cromwell.

Charles II, upon his return to power, vengefully had Guthrie murdered for his huge support of Oliver Cromwell and his advocacy for Presbyterianism. At Edinburgh Cross Guthrie was hanged screaming, "The Covenants! The Covenants! They shall yet be Scotland's reviving!")

Prior to James becoming of age to accept the crown of Scotland, four different regents, including the Earl of Moray known as the kind regent, ruled on his behalf. In

1578 James at age thirteen, finally, began his reign as King of Scotland and used Stirling Castle as his royal residence.

Early in young James' reign, several notorious Papish Dukes won the young King's close friendship and confidence. They greatly influenced young James' thinking, especially his rejection of Scotland's Presbyterian faith. His close circle of Dukes enhanced their position by supporting the young King's notion of "Kingly Power".

James I believed God had appointed him to the Scottish throne and that he only had to answer to God. Unfortunately, James' son Charles I, followed by James' grandsons, Charles II and James II, ascended the throne and continued James I's engrained "Kingly Right" attitude. For many years the Stuart's Kingly Rights adversely affected the freedom and liberties of subjects in the British Isles and colonial America. Under their "Kingly Right" philosophy, the King is God's supreme representative on earth and possesses the power to compel obedience and submission in God's name.

The Stuarts' Kingly Right theory justified the English monarch to control his subject's hearts and minds, to use police force, even to impose the death penalty as to religious beliefs and practices that contradicted those of the Anglican Church.

James I also expressed interest to be God's divine representative in charge of the Presbyterian Church. The Presbytery informed James that only God was their "Supreme Being" and only God could head their Presbyterian faith. Upon this rejection, James was furious and soon began his persecution of the Presbyterians. He turned his back on many of his former Scottish supporters.

James was unduly influenced by his circle of many Anglican friends and recognized that the Anglican Church supported the political expediency of his "Kingly Rights". He desired to head Scotland's ecclesiastical affairs. He cleverly saw that by choosing the Anglican Church as the

Church of England, with its many Catholic trappings, he could easily control the religious affairs of Scotland. He as King replaced the Pope and was able to control ecclesiastical revenues to support his extravagant living style. James recognized that by controlling the religious affairs of Scotland he could control Scotland's general assembly and, thereby, dominate all political and religious decisions.

In seeking to gain control of Scotland's ecclesiastical matters, James imposed his "King Craft". He bribed many Presbyterian ministers to become Anglican bishops. However, many ministers, including John Gillespie and Patrick Simson, refused James' financial incentives. Even though James was a master of manipulation, he soon discovered that the Presbyterian leaders were mostly loyal to their Church. These devout ministers could not be easily used as a mechanism by the Crown to control political and religious outcomes for personal gain through the inducement of ecclesiastical revenues.

The Gillespies, Simsons, Melvilles, were appalled when Patrick Adamson, the Archbishop of St. Andrews, who was Minister Simson's uncle, joined Scotland's close circle of King James' Anglican advisors. King James ordered Scotland's ministers to acknowledge the authority of Adamson as arch-bishop of St. Andrews, or lose their benefices. Patrick Simpson, even though Adamson was his uncle, opposed James' power usurpation.

Soon James' Parliament of selected aristocratic Anglicans undermined the independence of the Presbyterian Church. James declared before any religious service was held that the Church had to obtain the Crown's approval. The Presbyterians labeled these malicious acts of the Crown as the "Black Acts".

The tide continued to turn against the Presbyterians. Their Kirk was dreadfully affected when James appointed many Anglicans as his Dukes and Archbishops. His hand-picked scoundrels ordered the imprisonment and murder of many Presbyterians and their devoted ministers.

In 1592 the second "Earl of Moray", a leading Protestant, was murdered by George Gordon the Earl of Huntley, a devoted Catholic. Moray, a Presbyterian, was a member of Scotland's powerful Campbell clan, and the son of the first Earl of Moray. The first Earl of Moray was Mary Queen of Scots' half-brother. She had granted the title "Earl of Moray". Adding to the mystery surrounding Moray's murders were rumors that King James suspected his wife Queen Anne was having a romantic relationship with this dashing and handsome Moray.

George Gordon, sixth Earl of Huntley, was especially loyal to the Catholic cause. The Gordon Clan had a reputation for violence in Scotland. These two powerful Scottish families had much animosity; thus, Moray's death reopened the Campbell- Gordon family feud.

Moray harassed Gordon on the latter's estate. To make the situation worse, Gordon befriended Bothwell whose behavior terrified King James and many among his court in Edinburgh. When Clan warfare reopened between the Gordons and Campbells, King James attempted to intervene and brought both Earls to Edinburgh. His intervention failed to settle their dispute.

Fighting continued and Huntley returned to the King in Edinburgh. Cleverly, Moray stayed just across the Forth in the safety of his mother's estate. Meanwhile James commissioned Huntley to arrest Bothwell. During his assignment to arrest Bothwell, he decided to visit Moray at the Campbell estate to request that Moray return to Edinburgh. During Huntley's discussions with Moray at the Campbell estate, Huntley killed Moray on the pretext that he was resisting arrest.

Two days later, John Campbell was killed. Did the

Huntley's intend to kill other members of the Campbell family as well? What part did King James play in these Huntley murders? The King, conveniently, claimed he was away hunting, with Queen Anne, during the Huntley fights with the Campbells. Suspiciously, the King took little action against Huntley and only placed him under house arrest for a few days.

Using the Catholic killing of a Presbyterian as a political opportunity, the Presbyterians pushed their "Golden Act" legislature through Scotland's parliament. This legislation favored Presbyterianism, rejected Catholicism, and approved synods and Presbyteries. When infuriated Puritans convinced the Church of Scotland to ex-communicate Huntley, James became enraged.

Several weeks following Huntley's murderous act, Patrick Simson, minister of Sterling's Holy Rude, preached before King James with his sermon based on Genesis-4:9 :"The Lord asked Cain where is thy brother Abel. Cain denied being his brother's keeper" (Cain was the world's first murderer and Abel the first martyr.)

Simson turned to King James," I assure you, the Lord will ask you, King James, where is thy Earl of Moray". Furious, James, stood up, thrust his hand in anger toward Minister Simson, and screamed, "Master Patrick, as my friend and Chaplain, my door is never closed to you!"

Following Minister Simson's sermon, King James sauntered, so kingly, to the pulpit. The King summoned Minister Simson to discuss Huntley's murderous act up the hill in his private palace chambers in Stirling Castle. The next day, Reverend Patrick Simson paid a visit to the King. He proudly lugged his highly prized Geneva Bible with his many marginal notations against kingly rights under his arm. Up the steep and winding hill, to Stirling Castle, he climbed to discuss Huntley's attack on Moray with King James in his private Palace Chambers. Minister Simson, with his friendly and especially charming personality, was, after several hours, seen whistling and strolling leisurely down from Stirling Castle. Many believed his return alive would be impossible. Obviously, Simson's ministry with King James and his royal court, especially supported by the influence of the "Countess of Mar", had made lasting friendship. He established much respect and rapport with King James.

(Minister Patrick Simpson Revered His Geneva Bible)

Throughout his life, Minister Simson, with his charisma was very moderate, peaceable, and especially charitable. All through Scotland, everyone respected and adored his preaching. Simson retained the favor and admiration of King James throughout his many years of preaching before him and his royal court.

In 1598 Simson warned King James about idolatry.

On another occasion he admonished the King for patronizing a manifest that breached divine laws. Following Simson's sermon on divine laws, James leisurely walked to the pulpit and exclaimed in an especially friendly manner, "As my friend and minister I wisely urge you not to meddle in my philosophy of "Kingly Rights" relative to "Divine Laws of my Kingdom."

King James had much respect for Minister Simson and held the minister in high regard even though Simson preached continually in favor of Presbyterianism. Throughout the Stirling countryside, many treasured Minister Simson's preaching. These included members of King James' court including James' cousin, the "Countess of Mar." She had fostered James at Stirling castle and often counseled him. The Countess and her charming daughter, Lady Erskine, fondly viewed minister Simson as their spiritual father. The Countess, through her friendship with minister Simson and under his personal guidance, became an ally of many persecuted Presbyterians.

Her husband, the" Earl of Mar," like King James, was educated by John Buchannan. The Earl was especially influential with James. During their instruction by Buchannan the two had formed a special bond.

King James in 1601 sent the Earl on a special goodwill mission to London to meet with Robert Cecil and other members of Elizabeth's Royal Court. Robert Cecil, the son of William Cecil, had become Secretary of State following Walsingham's death. The Earl of Mar and Cecil convinced the childless Queen Elizabeth that her nephew, James , should be her successor.

Scotland's Puritans became more and more frustrated over King James' ignoring their religious rights to worship freely as Presbyterians. Scotland's theologians in 1596 selected a delegation of Andrew Melville, Patrick Simson, and several other leading theologians, to meet with James at Edinburgh Castle. Melville confronted the King like a lion in a cage. They informed King James, "When you King James replaced the Presbyterian Church and Covenant you assumed a power and authority which only belongs to God. King James, God is our only spiritual King and is head of our Church. Your Popery replaced Christ which mocked and wrecked God's true religion." Melville was unrelenting, "Even though you are King over men, you are only God's silly vassal." Melville's words greatly infuriated King James. Wisely, Melville and his Presbyterian delegation hastily departed Edinburgh to escape the King's wrath.

In April of 1603 following the death of Queen Elizabeth, England, through the recommendations of William Cecil and with strenuous objections from many Presbyterians, selected James Stuart, son of Mary Queen of Scots, to be King of England.

James Stuart now ruled both Scotland and England, as a "United Kingdom". James was especially astonished when he inherited the wealth of England. When he traveled to London for his crowning, James nearly knighted everyone from Edinburgh Castle to Westminster Abbey. James rode ever so leisurely off the beaten path on his way to London to ensure that Queen Elizabeth's funeral procession had long ended. Prior to James leaving Edinburgh, Presbyterian ministers drafted a petition that included over a thousand signatures. This Millenary Petition to King James listed their many ecclesiastical concerns. The word *Millenary* is derived from the Latin word meaning thousand.

Sir Walter Raleigh was a devout Presbyterian and was furious over the selection of James as King; especially, since James over the years in Scotland had subverted Scotland's Presbyterian religion and Kirk. Frustrated, Raleigh became involved in a plot, known as the Main plot, to remove James from the throne. For his part in the Main Plot against King James, Raleigh was tried and convicted of treason. King James spared his life but imprisoned Raleigh in the Tower of London.

In 1616 Raleigh was released to lead an expedition to Venezuela in search of El Dorado, the lost city of gold. Unable to resist the temptations of Spanish loot, Raleigh's expedition attacked the outpost of San Tome on the Orinoco River. He sacked the town and killed many Spaniards. During his expedition his son, Watt Raleigh, was killed by the Spaniards.

When Raleigh returned from his voyage, the Spanish ambassador was outraged. He demanded that Raleigh be sentenced to death. To keep peace with Spain, King James ordered the beheading of the renowned English explorer who had saved England from the onslaught of the Spanish Armada. Raleigh, also, had gallantly led the founding of English colonies in America on behalf of the English Crown.

Sir Walter Raleigh's beheading by James was influenced by James' son Charles, who was married to Maria, a Spanish Infante, i.e. a daughter of a King who is not heir to his throne. Charles marriage to Maria was known in England as the "Spanish match." James supported Charles' marriage to Spanish royalty to pacify Spain and prevent the costs of further conflict with Spain. Raleigh's beheading proved later not to have any influence on maintaining peaceful relations with Spain. A wiser decision, relative to Raleigh, would have been for James to have protected Raleigh and used his expert seamanship for defense against the continual dangers of the Spaniards.

In 1604 King James lured Scotland's theologians to Hampton Court, his Royal Palace along the Thames River, to discuss support for their Presbyterian doctrine. The Presbyterians earlier had provided their millenary petition of concerns to King James as he rode out of Edinburgh on his way to his coronation in London. Their demands included the abolition of religious confirmation, wedding rings, and the word priest in their religious doctrine. King James discussed everything but religious doctrine with these unwavering Presbyterians. James, again, proved he was a master of manipulation.

Even though James' Hampton Court assembly did not resolve any theological issues for Scotland's determined Puritans, the conference had huge accomplishments. Disappointed in King James' expressing little interest in upholding Scotland's Kirks, John Reynolds and four leading Scottish theologians requested that the Bible, God's Word, be translated into English from the Greek and Hebrew scripture. James, much aware of the political benefit to him, as well as an opportunity to receive a great deal of recognition, authorized the enormous task of accurately translating the New and Old Testaments into English.

King James agreed and assembled a large commission of England's greatest scholars led by the brilliant Lancelot Andrews, Dean of Westminster. They were to interpret the ancient biblical writings of Greek, Hebrew, and Aramaic in order to reflect accurately God's Word into English.

James informed his scholars that the Puritan's influence was to be limited. Fortunately, the Puritans earlier translated the Bible into their Geneva version. The Puritans ensured that several copies of their cherished Geneva Bible were readily available to guide James' scholars as they worked diligently over years to draft what remains today as the King James Bible.

The Catholic Church feared that its Douay Bible would be avoided with a more understandable language of the era; thus, lessening Catholic influence on Christianity. The Catholic Church was adamantly against King James' translation. The Protestants included notes in the preface regarding Catholic opposition to King James' crowning achievement. The King James Bible, throughout the centuries, has served to shape the English language, to support the power of Kings, and to reaffirm individual freedom of will.

England's many Anglican Bishops continued to influence King James and he became even more determined to destabilize Scotland's Presbyterian religion and Kirk. In desperation, Patrick Simson drafted a protest for leading Scottish theologians to present to King James, at Perth, during the 1606 General Assembly of the Scottish Parliament. Among the first signatories were Andrew Melville and John Gillespie minister of Kirkcaldy. King James ignored Simson's petition and accused the six ministers of treason.

Simson attended the trial of his six true theologian friends, which was held at Linlithgow just west of Edinburgh. Minister Simson supported his helpless theologian friends by every means within his power. Showing no mercy, King James unleashed harsh punishment on these innocent ministers and in 1607 he imprisoned John Welsh, Knox's son in-law, in a dungeon at the Castle of Blackness. James banished Robert Bruce to Inverness, a no- man's land, and imprisoned Andrew Melville in the Tower of London.

Following Andrew Melville's imprisonment in the Tower of London, Simson raised a subscription for his release. Meanwhile, again as a bribe in appeasement, James offered Presbyterian ministers a bishopric with a lifetime ecclesiastical Anglican pension. Robert Bruce and Patrick Simpson were among the faithful Presbyterian ministers who refused such financial incentives to betray their Presbyterian faith.

With leading ministers imprisoned or banished, James attempted to minimalize the Presbyterian religion in Scotland and in 1610 he audaciously assembled a church court, the Glasgow Assembly, and introduced a prelatic church government. His bishops took control over

Scotland's religious affairs and were empowered as moderators of diocesan synods and excommunicators with authority to absolve or punish offenders. Within their powers were ordination and disposal of ministers

Under increasing pressure from Anglican Bishops, King James, over the last quarter of the 16th century, undermined Presbyterianism's ascendance. His defilement increased as the 17th century dawned and for the next decade Scotland's Presbyterians were faced with escalating difficulty to sustain their religious freedom. King James, with his Anglican supporters, forced the Crown's Anglican religion upon the Scots and overpowered Scotland's Presbyterian faith.

Presbyterian theologians, including Patrick Simson, sought to preserve Calvinistic doctrine. These devout Presbyterians deemed that government should be conducted by the word of God literally from the Bible without Douay Bible version edits by Rome. They believed their Kirk should control their local religious activity without the interference from Government or a priest to act as a mandatory intermediary to enable communication with God. Through the support of their Kirk, they steadfastly supported their governing philosophy that common man should control Government based on policies and regulations established by the rule of law, not that of man. Until his death, King James continued to undermine religious freedom from Anglicanism.

Through his Anglican hierarchy, James preserved his monarchial supremacy that protected England's top down religious, social, governmental power structure. The Puritans viewed James' Anglican Church as a mere successor to the repressive Catholic Church monolith with much influence from Catholic tradition. James, as the King of England, had forced his will upon the populace in a similar fashion as the popes of Rome had for centuries.

Scotland's many renowned Presbyterians,

especially Gillespie, Simson, and Melville died frustrated and were broken-hearted by King James' rejection of his Presbyterian upbringing by his Scottish regents.

During the 1606 Perth Parliament, John Gillespie and his father-in-law, Patrick Simson, made their last desperate stand against James' mandated Anglican ceremonies. The Perth General Assembly was Scotland's last assembly of their Kirk for twenty years. Scotland's next Parliamentary Church Assembly would be their famous 1638 Glasgow Assembly, led by Alexander Henderson, in which Patrick Simpson's grandson, George Gillespie, was destined to play a vital role.

King James I during his reign established the Anglican Church as the Church of England. His Kingly political/religious rights philosophy so atrociously destroyed the legendary ecclesiastical efforts of John Knox, John Gillespie, Andrew Melville, Patrick Simson, and other brave, determined, Scottish theologians. These devoted religious leaders had struggled and fought long and hard for religious and political freedom so as to maintain Presbyterianism as a faith. James' Anglican followers confiscated and burned all copies of the Presbyterian Covenant that they could find.

In retrospect, James with his Anglican Church continued to cast aside indulgences and other introduced Christian aberrations of the Catholic Church that existed in England over many centuries. Obviously, the Catholics were not pleased with his political/religious beliefs and attempted on several occasions, such as the "Gunpowder Plot" of Guy Fawkes, to murder King James.

Chapter 4
King Charles I and the Presbyterian/Covenanter Revolution

Following the reign of James I in 1625 his son Charles I was crowned King of England. Charles, to fulfill his father's dreams, insisted on Great Britain becoming a united kingdom with one uniform religion, i.e. the Anglican Church. For this purpose, he imposed his "Book of Common Prayer" and his appointed loyal bishops for control.

In reaction, Parliament insisted through their "Magna Carta" that all subjects possess basic human rights, which the King is bound to honor. Parliament presented Charles with their "Petition of Right" and he so merrily disregarded their grievances.

In 1627 King Charles' first attempt to organize a United Kingdom was a fiasco when England entered the Thirty Years War with France. King Charles' French Huguenot relief expedition, led by the Duke of Buckingham, suffered defeat by Catholic forces. The British Parliament opened impeachment against the Duke and King Charles abolished his Parliament. After King Charles saved his favorite Duke by closing Parliament, the Parliament accused King Charles of favoring his Anglican Bishops.

For the next decade, Charles ruled without a Parliament which limited his ability to raise revenue to manage his kingdom. Under his so-called personal rule, he imposed the Anglican Church's sacraments and his authoritarian Bishops.

Anglicans supported by the Crown attempted to force the faithful Presbyterians to attend the Anglican Church's ceremonies. The Anglicans made large incomes from their Church tithes.

Scotland, which loathed and distrusted Charles I,

rebelled and began their Presbyterian revolution. Charles, in frustration, withdrew his Anglican prayer book. In November 1638 Charles summoned a General Assembly meeting in Glasgow to resolve religious affairs. Scotland's Parliament used King Charles' General Assembly to declare his prayer book and Bishop appointments to be unlawful. King Charles demanded furiously that the assembly be disbanded, but the Scots refused.

Scotland's 1638 General Assembly was supported by strong-minded lay elders and determined ministers of the Kirk. They swept away the Crown's Anglican liturgy and bishops' rule that the Stuarts had enforced over the last forty years. Scotland, forever, referred to these brave freedom-loving Presbyterians as Covenanters.

Scotland's Presbyterians were led by their renowned theologians, including brothers Patrick and George Gillespie, Samuel Rutherford, Alexander Henderson, and Robert Baille. They furiously resisted King Charles imposing his Anglican liturgy. The brave Presbyterian ministers preached and published numerous sermons against the forced rule of the English Anglican Church. In 1635 Scotland's renowned Presbyterian ministers wrote, with the legal assistance of Scottish judge Archibald Johnston, their new "National Covenant".

In 1638 over 60,000 Scottish Covenanters, many weeping due to their deep emotion, patiently waited for several days in long lines at their parishes all across Scotland to sign their National Covenant. Thousands of joyful Covenanters demonstrated their strong anguish toward the Crown and signed their legendary calfskin parchments which were inscribed with their blood.

Scotland's ministers including Rutherford, Henderson and the Gillespies led many thousands of Covenanters assembled at Greyfriar Church and throughout Scotland to sign Scotland's Covenant.

Scotland's Covenant

(Education Scotland –Terms of Open Government License)
- SIGNING OF SCOTLAND'S COVENANT AT
GREYFRIARS-

(Standing on bench, Samuel Rutherford expounds on the importance of signing Scotland's Covenant)

Greyfriar Church was consecrated in 1620. This was the same year the Pilgrims sailed to America aboard their Mayflower sailing vessel to establish their Puritan Church at Plymouth Rock. Greyfriar is Scotland's first free church. To commemorate the occasion the U.S. Congress presented an American flag in 1970 to Greyfriar's Kirk. These humble Puritans migrated to America aboard their Mayflower sailing craft and created a new society. Upon arrival in America they drafted their Covenant. Their Government, with laws of the land, was so successful that 40,000 more Puritans emigrated from England and settled in their American colony.

Meanwhile, Charles with his continuing military threats enraged the Scots. With their engrained fighting spirit akin to that of William Wallace and Robert Bruce they confronted King Charles' military might. Charles frantically recalled the English Parliament that he had dismissed eleven years earlier. Charles appointed a new Parliament and ordered Parliament to raise funds critically needed to support the escalating battles with the Covenanters. The new Parliament proved even more hostile to King Charles and revolted. Charles' rule became chaotic and civil war threatened. Frantically, King Charles raised his militia to face the mighty Covenanter Scottish Army and the so-called Bishops Wars began.

In 1639 King Charles' royal militia struggled to end the Scottish rebellion. The Covenanters commanded by Leslie overwhelmed Charles' forces and they forced King Charles to accept a Scottish truce known as the Pacification of Berwick or the" Treaty of Berwick."

Scottish Judge Archibald Johnston wrote the terms of the Berwick Treaty to ensure the most favorable political and religious rights were obtained for the citizens of Scotland.

The Berwick Treaty ended the first Bishop War. Charles was determined to continue his Anglican liturgy campaign that resulted in England's second Bishop War. The Covenanters again defeated Charles' royal forces at Kelso and they forced Charles into another truce. This time Charles promised the faithful Covenanters freedom of religion. Throughout the Bishop Wars, the Covenanters were continually in danger of loss of life, but they continued to fight for parliamentary and religious rights.

A year later in 1640, King Charles continued his attack on the Protestants. Again, the Scottish militia drove back the King's royalists. With the Scots capture of New Castle, the Covenanters forced King Charles to sign the Treaty of Ripon. Scotland's commissioners for the Ripon Treaty included Leslie, Campbell, Johnston, Rutherford and George Gillespie. These mighty Scotch theologian commissioners insisted upon Treaty provisions that required King Charles to honor the Covenanter's freedom to worship freely without Anglican religious sacraments and without his imposition of bishops. Charles guaranteed that the Presbyterian Church would be the National Church of Scotland. Treaty terms also specified that Scotland would be granted Northumberland, the counties of Durham and New Castle, and 850 pounds currency per day to maintain a Scottish militia in New Castle. For the moment, Scotland had King Charles on his knees and under their command.

Additional terms of the Ripon Treaty specified that Scotland would provide England four commissioners to introduce Presbyterianism to the English. They were to preach throughout London and the English countryside. The four Scottish theologians who were selected to sway the English into accepting Presbyterianism were Henderson, Blaire, George Gillespie and Baille. These four dedicated ministers preached daily before huge audiences at both the House of Lords and House of Commons. These mighty Scottish theologians also preached at a number of London's churches, including Saint Antholin, a medieval church in downtown London. Calvinist and English Puritans became more united every day in an overwhelming crusade to supersede episcopacy. George Gillespie, with his exhaustive preaching and his hard driven efforts to defeat Episcopalianism, became known as the Hammer.

During Scotland's Presbyterian Revolution, John Milton, as an independent, wrote many of his allegorical sonnets to portray the many political and religious turmoils of the era. Milton's famous work, Paradise Lost, reflects the historical details and characters of England and Scotland's religious upheavals. Milton particularly disliked George Gillespie's forceful preaching. In his sonnet composed as a "Tetrachordon" (musical combination of four notes), Milton disparaged Gillespie as the "hammer". During the famous Westminster Assembly, Milton spent many days listening intently to the debates of England and Scotland's renowned theologians. As a parliamentarian, Milton was especially fond of Cromwell's rhetorical skills. Cromwell selected Milton, due to his extensive knowledge of Latin and Italian, as his Secretary of Foreign Tongues.

In 1642 King Charles' belligerent actions instigated a civil war between his Royalists and Parliament in which Charles' Royal Militia at first drew a standoff against Parliament's troops. Parliament soon gained the support of the Scottish army after Parliament signed and agreed to terms of Scotland's Solemn League and Covenant, which included the Crown's continued acceptance of the Presbyterian Church.

With support of the unified Scottish Covenanters, the tide of battle changed in favor of Parliament. Now the English Parliament, led by Oliver Cromwell, with the enormous support of the Covenanter's militia, won crucial battles. Cromwell had been a long-time supporter of

Parliament and adamantly believed in Parliamentary rights as a reflection of the people's elected representatives.

In 1643 in the midst of Scotland and England's political and religious turmoil, England's Parliament was fed up with Charles' continual abusive religious and political antics. Seeking relief from Charles' unjust demands and his Royalist supporters, Parliament held a general assembly in Glasgow to discuss a military-religious alliance with the Scottish Presbyterians. Included with the religious terms of the alliance was unification of England's and Scotland's theology under a Presbyterian system of localized church governing bodies. At this special joint assembly, Scottish Covenanters and the Parliament, formalized their alliance, known as the "Solemn League and Covenant", for a military and religious union.

Solemn League and Covenant

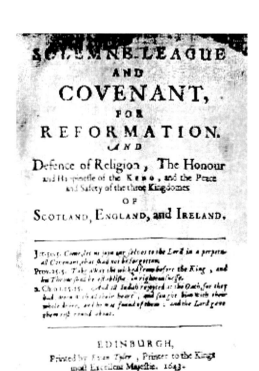

In 1644 at the battle of Marston Moor Cromwell led Parliamentary forces to a decisive victory that confirmed both his political and military skills. In 1645 Cromwell, under Sir Thomas Fairfax, destroyed the armies of King Charles I. Charles, with his Army in shambles, sought and gained protection from the Scottish Army. Charles was desperate. In 1647, he negotiated a new agreement with Scotland that provided freedom of religion and for the Presbyterian Church to be Scotland's national church.

Fighting continued between England's Parliamentarians commanded by Cromwell, and England's Royalists loyal to their King. Scotland under the leadership of Marquis of Montrose supported King Charles and his Royalists especially since Charles had promised Anglican Church members reform throughout England.

The Gillespie family, then headed by Patrick, adamantly advised the Covenanters, militarily led by Montrose, against forming an alliance with King Charles. He warned, "You should not trust the Stuart's!" Tragically, the signed promise of both Kings was no more than a mere piece of paper. Charles I was charged with treason and beheaded. Charles II, upon returning from France to regain the throne, turned his back on his faithful Covenanter supporters. He, so coldheartedly, betrayed the humble Presbyterians who saved him from being slaughtered by Cromwell.

Sadly, many of the Covenanters neither failed to heed any of their warnings of royal political perfidy nor sought to gain guarantees to ensure fairness from Charles II.

(When Cromwell gained control of England, Patrick Gillespie became Cromwell's most trusted Scottish ally. This Gillespie had enormous influence on Cromwell's policies concerning religious affairs within Scotland.)

(The Westminster Assembly produced the documents that are today's major confessional Standards of the Presbyterian faith. A separate chapter is devoted to George Gillespie as one of the leading Scottish theologians and moderator of the famous Westminster Assembly. This assembly was orchestrated and approved by England's long parliament in conjunction with the religiously driven Covenanters without the approval of King Charles. The parliament's main objective in this era of Charles' chaotic struggles with England and Scotland's Parliament was to restructure the Church of England.)

Chapter 5
Presbyterian Minister George Gillespie and the Westminster Assembly of Divines

George Gillespie played a key role in the breakthrough for Presbyterian freedom from the Anglican Church and for religious liberty. Gillespie, the renowned Scottish theologian, led the Westminster Assembly for Scotland to establish firmly the Presbyterian Confessional Standards.

(Scotland's famous, Presbyterian, evangelist George Gillespie was the great, great grandfather of U.S. Congressman James Gillespie from Duplin, North Carolina, and North Carolina State Senator Daniel Gillespie and his brother John from Alamance County. John and Daniel adamantly supported Alamance County's 1770 "Regulator Battle" against the corruptions of colonial Governor Tryon.)

George Gillespie is the grandson of Patrick Simpson who served as minister to King James I and his royal court during James' residency at Stirling Castle, and the son of Reverend John Gillespie a leading theologian during Scotland's first reformation. George Gillespie was born in 1613 in Kirkcaldy, Fife Scotland, which borders the north shore of the Firth of Forth River. The town of Kirkcaldy is the birthplace for a number of renowned Scotsmen, including Adam Smith whom the world recognizes as the "father of modern economics."

The County of Fife was the center of Scotland's 16th and 17th century ecclesiastical reformation. County Fife was also the birthplace for many leading Scottish theologians, including Richard Cameron, and Samuel Rutherford. It was home of the Leslie family who led the Covenanter victories against Charles I's Royalist army at Marston Moor. These proud Puritans often referred to their homeland as the "Kingdom of Fife". Around the Fife countryside, many freedom loving Scottish families like the Camerons, Bruces, Simsons, Gillespies and Leslies proudly voiced a spirit of independence. These Scots believed in religious and political freedom and were motivated by personal honor, justice for the common man and by rule of law.

Reverend John Gillespie served as minister of Kirkcaldy's historic parish known as the Old Kirk Church on Kirk Wynd. The Church was sanctified by Bishop Berham of St. Andrews in 1244. During Scotland's first reformation, John Gillespie furthered the Presbyterian faith with his thundering sermons during his ministry for the "Old Kirk Wynd".

Among the treasures of this historic Kirk, with a medieval Norman tower erected at one end, are George Gillespie's portrait in a stained glass window and his churchyard memorial. George Gillespie's portrait fills the window inside the south porch and his memorial stone rests near the south porch wall.

Following the return of King Charles II from France to regain the English Crown, Charles ordered Archbishop Sharpe to destroy Gillespie's plaque commemorating his devoted efforts in the Covenanters' freedom movement. Fortunately, George Gillespie's grandson re-erected the Gillespie historical memorial, which today is so dear to Scotland in remembrance of the Covenanters reformation and freedom crusade.

**(Famed Kirkcaldy Kirk Wynd with Gillespie's
Memorial Stained Window)**

Other famous Presbyterian Covenanters honored
with stained glass windows in Kirkcaldy's famous Kirk are
Alexander Henderson and John Knox.

As a youth, George Gillespie exhibited great
knowledge and capability for the ministry. He, like his
mentor and close friend Samuel Rutherford, received his
Doctorate of Divinity from Saint Andrews Seminary. Saint
Andrews, in Northeast Fife, was a long carriage ride to the
Gillespie's Kirkcaldy home. Both George and his brother
Patrick made the ride to St Andrews many times to earn
their respective degrees. The Gillespie boys' great uncle,
Patrick Adamson, earlier served as the Archbishop of Saint
Andrews.

Saint Andrew Seminary educated a number of well-
known Scots-Irish Presbyterian ministers, including John
Witherspoon who brought his family to America to serve as
the President of the Seminary College of New Jersey which

is today Princeton University. Many American colonial leaders received their degrees from St. Andrews, including Dr. Benjamin Franklin.

After George Gillespie received his Doctorate of Divinity he soon married Margaret Murray. The Gillespies raised three sons Robert, George, and Archibald and a daughter Elizabeth. His elder son Robert became a leading Presbyterian Covenanter during the reign of King Charles II. In 1673 Charles imprisoned Minister Robert Gillespie in Scotland's Bass Rock Prison for preaching the Presbyterian faith at conventicles throughout the Scottish countryside.

In 1710 one of Robert's sons, George was graduated with Cotton Mather from Glasgow University. In 1712 through Mather's recommendations and the support of Glasgow's Dean of Divinity, George Gillespie sailed to Boston to support Mather and America's Presbytery. The George Gillespie family members of America were all devout Presbyterians and were devoted to their Church. They deeply believed that the Church must have a congregational organization and a community-meeting place for discussing and solving everyday problems and concerns. Social, cultural, and religious values were deeply rooted in the thousands of Scots-Irish Presbyterians who emigrated to America with steadfast belief in religious and political freedom.

Presbyterians, supported by their Kirk, firmly believed they had the right of worship of their choice. Their individualistic philosophy, through their Kirk, resulted in establishing policies and laws from the bottom up.

During the 1630s, when King Charles I imposed his Anglican liturgy on the British Isles, George Gillespie displayed his immense theological knowledge by responding directly to the Crown's attempts to impose Anglican liturgy on the Presbyterians of Scotland. In 1637 George Gillespie published, "A Dispute against the English-Popish Ceremonies Obtruded upon the Church of

Scotland." George's manuscript attacked Anglican liturgy, and directly criticized the Crown for imposing Anglican liturgy and openly criticized the Crown for imposing their Anglican religion upon Scotland.

George Gillespie's writing angered King Charles and his Anglican supporters. In order to protect Gillespie from the King's wrath, Gillespie's Presbyterian associates published his religious manuscript in Leiden, Holland. The Covenanters secretly smuggled Gillespie's manuscript back to Scotland. When Gillespie's writing arrived in Scotland, it was widely distributed and read throughout the land.

Samuel Rutherford, a residing professor at St. Andrews, and George Gillespie became closest of friends. Rutherford, over the years, like Gillespie, wrote influential ecclesiastical manuscripts. One of his more famous books is "Lex Rex", i.e. Law is King. He wrote this brilliant manuscript during his committed service as an advisor to the Westminster Assembly proceedings. Rutherford's writing provided a guideline for America's Republic. It served as a model for future civil government and provided basic principles for the British and America's Constitutional Law. The writing accurately expressed the Presbyterian ruling philosophy and masterfully defended the Covenanters' political principles of self-reliance in clashes with King Charles I.

The main theme of Rutherford's celebrated manuscript "Lex Rex" was borrowed centuries later by American president Abraham Lincoln in his legendary Gettysburg address. Lincoln quoted Rutherford's cherished governmental ideal, "Of the people, by the people, for the people".

The many thousand Scots-Irish who emigrated from Ulster to America from the early to mid- 18th century firmly believed in Rutherford's philosophical guideline, "the power of the people must be above the power of the President and the legislators the people so duly elect."

Rutherford set forth that the liberty and rights of people must be preserved relative to the law and the government. His liberty and rights philosophy is evident in the Scots-Irish demands that America's Constitution and Bill of Rights must protect the common man." *Lex Rex"* advocated, "People are King, and people are from God; true sovereignty belongs to God not the people. The power of the people is above the power of the King, and Parliament has greater power than the King." Rutherford firmly believed, "People appoint the King to be their servant".

John Coffey's book, "Politics Religion and the British Revolutions," provides an excellent portrayal of the brilliance of Rutherford's mind. Rutherford's many letters to fellow ministers and parishioners greatly inspired theology throughout Scotland and encouraged the writing of a song, "The Sands of Time are Sinking." Widely read, Rutherford's letters reflected Scotland's hardships and theological philosophy. The common Scottish villagers especially cherished his philosophy of kindness towards the every-day man.

George Gillespie maintained a close personal contact with Rutherford throughout their famous work for the Presbytery. After receiving his Doctor of Divinity from St. Andrews, George Gillespie refused to be ordained by an Anglican bishop. Thus for a brief period, he was unable to minister. In 1638 Gillespie was finally ordained by Scotland's Presbyterian Church. George was Scotland's first minister, during the reign of King Charles I, to be ordained with total disregard to Charles' Anglican Church and many bishops.

A few months later during the Glasgow Assembly, George Gillespie, Alexander Henderson, and Samuel Rutherford were instrumental in re-establishing the governing body of the Presbyterian Church. These Scottish ministers were ever-determined that Scotland had freedom of religion that was introduced in the first reformation in mid-1500s by John Knox and fellow theologians. George Gillespie's father, John Gillespie and grandfather Patrick Simson, preached vigorously during Scotland's first reformation in support of Presbyterianism.

George Gillespie, during his brief life of thirty-six years, wrote a number of evangelistic works, including "Aaron's Rod Blossoming". This publication advocated the separation of church and state. It was a direct rebuttal to the King's imposed Anglican liturgy and prayer book.

In 1640, the Scottish Commission of Estates recognized young Gillespie's enormous abilities and selected George as one of Scotland's representatives to the Treaty of Ripon. Gillespie, Leslie, Campbell, and Johnston served as Scottish Covenanter representatives to Treaty negotiations. Their diplomacy and intellect upheld Scotland's ecclesiastical rights and ended England's Second Bishop War. This conflict ending treaty was a major setback for Charles I with its humiliating terms that surrendered England's Northumberland and County Durham to Scotland.

Shortly after signing their "Solemn League and Covenant", members of Scotland's and England's Parliaments selected the greatest theologians to serve in their historically significant Westminster Assembly. They were faced with a formidable task, the development of a religious philosophy agreeable to both the English and Scottish common man. This legendary assembly met from 1643 through 1649 and produced confessional standards for the Presbyterian faith that included: the Westminster Confession of Faith, the Westminster Larger Catechism, the Westminster Shorter Catechism, and the directory of Public Worship.

To support their theological views in this legendary assembly, Scotland elected the young and vibrant George Gillespie as their lead spokesman. His theologian friends,

Samuel Rutherford, Alexander Henderson, and Robert Baille provided much assistance to George Gillespie during his nine challenging years of theological assembly meetings. These Scottish theologians ensured Scotland's Presbyterian liturgy was well supported. George, at age thirty, brilliantly led the assembly debates to provide the vindication of their Church's rule of discipline.

During the Westminster Assembly, Oliver Cromwell, as a Congregationalist, visited the proceedings on a number of occasions to listen to the inspired theological debate. The distinguished members of the Assembly represented four main religious beliefs: Episcopacy, Presbyterianism, Erastianism, and Congregationalism. Scotland ensured that the assembly had a large number of Presbyterians.

During the Assembly, Rutherford stated, "Recognizing Gillespie's astonishing theological work it appears that God has provided Gillespie, as a prophet to us, to ensure that our Presbyterian doctrine is heard and supported by the Assembly. Reverend George Gillespie without a doubt is one of the most remarkable statesmen and ministers that God has ever given to Scotland and the world".

Throughout the assembly, Scotland's great theologians told many stories of young Gillespie's debating powers. During the proceedings, one of England's most famous lawyers and greatest orators, John Selden, made an incredible and overwhelming speech supporting Erastianism, (i.e. the state authority over the church and religion). No one, neither friend nor foe, believed Selden's noble speech was answerable. One after the other of the Constitutional and Evangelical assembly members tried desperately but was unable to respond to Selden's renowned speech. Rutherford, George's dearest friend sitting next to George, quietly whispered, "Rise George, defend Scotland's church which Christ has purchased with his holy blood." George slowly rose and began his most astounding and brilliant, response that totally overwhelmed Selden and the entire Westminster Assembly.

Selden, much exasperated, exclaimed, "That young man with his oratorical skills and theological knowledge, the greatest I have ever heard, has swept away all my learning and labor for the last ten years of my life". Selden and several other assembly members, at their first opportunity, rushed over to George's chair to gain a glimpse of such a renowned speech. Selden in total amazement exclaimed, "Gillespie has only scribbled on his small note pad---**God Is King**"--- unbelievable!"

(Painting by John Rogers Herbert of Westminster Assembly - Gillespie, red hair with hand near Chin, politely enduring Selden's inexhaustible speech on Erastianism)

Gillespie was exceedingly influential in publishing the Westminster Confession that provided today's key liturgy guidelines and Catechisms for the Presbyterian faith. His theological knowledge and writing skills were essential in setting forth the Confession that is today's guiding light for all Presbyterians.

The Westminster Confession, which George Gillespie was so influential in writing, contains and illuminates many of the ideals upon which America was established. Its influence on America's founding is vast. The Confession discusses the relationship between Church and State and stresses the need for voluntary assent in religious faith.

America's first four Universities, i.e. Harvard, William and Mary, Yale and Princeton, which were initially seminaries, required their students to be well versed in the Westminster Confessions. Daily recitations with memorization of the Confession and Catechism were an integral part of the University curriculum. James Madison, as a student at Princeton, was well versed in the Westminster Confession. America considers Madison as the father of the U.S. Constitution including the First Amendment. The Confession of Faith supported the First Amendment's freedom of religion which ensures Americans' voluntary assent in religious expression.

Second only to the Bible's distribution, the shorter Catechism of the Westminster Confession, during the pre-Revolutionary era, had over five million copies published. The Catechism, a central part of colonial education, was required in New England's schooling and became a central element of the "New England Primer"

The 120 distinguished assembly members met for nine years over a thousand times to complete their renowned Westminster "Confession of Faith" and Catechisms that became doctrinal standards for the Presbyterian Church.

On a number of occasions during George Gillespie's service as moderator of the Westminster Assembly, Westminster's House of Lords invited George Gillespie to preach before them in the Abbey Church at Westminster Cathedral. In 1647, Gillespie briefly left the Assembly to replace Alexander Henderson, who was deceased, as minister of Edinburgh's High Church in St. Giles Cathedral. John Knox had, so famously, served as minister to St. Giles. A few years following, George's brother Patrick also served as minister of St. Giles for a brief period.

- SAINT GILES CATHEDRAL -

Today, St. Giles is known as the "Mother Church of Presbyterianism".

Gillespie returned to the assembly in 1648. Recognizing his enormous knowledge of theology, the Assembly elected George Gillespie as their moderator and Chairman. His challenging responsibilities at the Assembly began to wear George down. Unknowingly, George was dying of Tuberculosis. In December 1648, at age 35, George Gillespie died at Kirkcaldy, his birthplace. During George's last days, Rutherford provided his dear fellow theologian, and close personal friend, with comfort and many encouraging words, remarking, "Young George in his brief life span accomplished much more than a multitude of godly grey-haired Pastors".

To honor George Gillespie, his portrait is ordained in a stain glass window of Kirkcaldy's Kirk where his father, Minister John Gillespie, preached his thundering sermons for many years.

George's younger brother, Patrick Gillespie, like George, steadfastly supported Scotland's Covenanter crusade. Patrick with the support of his faithful friend and staunch ally Archibald Johnston, a Scottish judge and one of the authors of Scotland's Covenant, vehemently opposed any Presbyterian allegiance to the Stuart Kings in their ongoing battle with Parliament. As true guardians of Scotland's Covenant, Johnston and Gillespie led Scotland's Western Association in their disputes against the Covenanters who were led by James Graham, 1st Marques of Montrose. Graham erroneously supported King Charles I with his Royal militia and Covenanter Scottish troops known as the Engagers.

Chapter 6
Cromwell's Protectorate and Parliamentary Rule

In August 1648, at the Battle of Preston, Oliver Cromwell and his Roundhead militia defeated Charles I's army composed of Royalists and Presbyterian Covenanters known as the Engagers. The victorious Scots released King Charles I to Cromwell who charged him with treason. King Charles was found guilty of high treason and Cromwell beheaded him on January 30, 1649, at the Palace of Whitehall.

When Cromwell and his army invaded Scotland, he advised the Covenanters to provide support to his army. Earlier in England's first civil war, the Presbyterian Covenanters led by General Leslie had been Cromwell's staunch allies. Cromwell appealed to Scotland's Engagers, "Please recognize the error of your Royal Alliance with the Stuart Kings- recognize that King Charles continues to deceive your beliefs and rights as Covenanters." Likewise, the Protestors led by Patrick Gillespie and Johnston counseled the many Presbyterians, "Please, as our long-time friends and fellow Presbyterian Covenanters we advise you not to support King Charles, and we emphasize the Stuarts are not to be trusted." They replied, "Would you insist we be skeptics in our religion?"

Ignoring Johnston's and Gillespie's warning, many Covenanters, organized as the "Engagers", continued to uphold their royal alliance with King Charles II. They insisted that he would honor his signature on Scotland's National Covenant for Scottish independence and religious freedom for Presbyterianism.

Meanwhile, Cromwell attacked Scotland and the Engagers and proceeded to crush these Covenanters at Dunbar. He captured ten thousand prisoners, and Scotland's capital, Edinburgh. Cromwell exiled many of the Scottish Covenanters to Massachusetts and Virginia in colonial America. Other prisoners were exiled to Barbados.

Patrick Gillespie, after the battle of Dunbar, supported an independent armed force, the Western Association, to oppose the Covenanter Engagers. The Engager's were led by Leslie in their support of Charles II. In bitter opposition to the Engagers, Patrick Gillespie authored the Western Remonstrance. This oppositional document was guided by the legal assistance of his faithful friend, Judge Johnston. Gillespie and Johnston, supported by their many remonstrant followers, presented their Western Remonstrance to Scotland's General Assembly. The document made charges against the Engagers, condemned their treaty with Charles, and declared that Scotland must not side with King Charles II against Cromwell.

The Engager Army led by Charles II made a last desperate attempt to re-capture London. The Cromwell army led by General Monck smashed the Scots militia at the battle of Worcester and destroyed the last remnants of the Royal Scottish Army.

Following defeat, the youthful twenty-one year old King Charles II faded into the English countryside with a small group of supporters. King Charles desperately sought a sailing vessel to France to join the comforts of his friends across the English Channel and to be with his mother, Queen Henrietta Maria.

Charles in the company of supporters, including Lord Wilmot, Lord Derby, and Charles Gilford, carefully crossed the English countryside heading toward Shropshire, a Catholic stronghold.

Charles and his companions had many close encounters with Cromwell's Parliamentary soldiers who were looking for the King. At Boscobel, a Royalist Colonel Carlis, who fought at Worchester, protected Charles from capture by hiding him overnight among the thick foliage of a large oak tree. Afraid to move, Charles and Colonel Carlis spent a very miserable night clinging to the limbs of their roost while soldiers passed underneath unaware of their whereabouts.

After six weeks, Charles reached Southampton where Lord Wilmot arranged for his passage to France through Royalist sympathizers on board a coal boat called the "Surprise". Finally, after avoiding capture over 615 miles of English countryside, Charles boarded his coal boat from Shoreham and sailed across the English Channel to France to the safety of King Louis XIV.

Throughout the first part of the 17th century, the Gillespie family had bitterly opposed the Stuarts and their Kingly Right of oppressive rule. Led by Patrick, the Gillespies welcomed Cromwell's conquest of England, especially his religious philosophy which was similar to that of Martin Luther. They greatly appreciated Cromwell's recognition of their Presbyterian faith, his great distaste for ritual ceremonies and decorations within the church as well as his vigorous objections to the authority of bishops and the King in religious affairs.

After their victory over King Charles, the triumphant Puritans took steps to turn England into an independent Democratic republic. The Puritans, led by Patrick Gillespie in Scotland, and Cromwell's faithful Roundheads in England, reformed the Government into a Commonwealth.

Patrick Gillespie diligently served Cromwell and was personally called to London to advise the "Lord Protector" on England's ecclesiastical affairs. Patrick was the first minister to pray publicly for Cromwell and all his proceedings at the High Church- St Giles in Edinburgh. No person in Scotland stood in greater favor with Cromwell or had more influence with the Lord Protector. For his devoted service and loyalty Cromwell appointed Patrick Gillespie as head of Glasgow University. From such leadership, Patrick obtained large sums from Cromwell for adding a number of buildings to the University. Among the beautiful architectural features, Gillespie added to the Glasgow University was a main gothic tower. Unfortunately, in 1863, all the beautiful Glasgow University architecture, built through the efforts of Patrick Gillespie, was lost when the University sold the old university site to the City of Glasgow Union Railway Company. Sadly, the railway chose to level the Glasgow University buildings and prepared the old campus for use as a site for their railroad operations.

In 1952, to honor Patrick Gillespie and twenty nine other renowned educators, Glasgow University for its 500th anniversary erected a beautiful memorial gate with the engraved names of Patrick Gillespie and twenty-nine other significant University officials.

Cromwell appointed Patrick Gillespie to remove Catholic influence and take over the management of each of Scotland's Universities. Using Glasgow as his management headquarters, where Scotland's Presbyterian National Covenant was chartered, Patrick Gillespie implemented his "Gillespie Charter" to lead Cromwell's purging of many papists who supported the Stuarts. Under the umbrella of Gillespie's Charter, the Architecture of Scotland's Universities was greatly improved. Gillespie, under the authority of Cromwell, replaced the principal professors of the Aberdeen and Edinburgh Universities. Gillespie appointed his close friend, John Roe, to head King's College of Aberdeen. Under John Roe's guidance, Patrick Simpson sponsored the construction of the magnificent Cromwell tower at Aberdeen in honor of the regent.

(King's College's Cromwell Tower Built under Gillespie's Charter)

At Edinburgh, Patrick Gillespie established a medical school. Today Edinburgh's medical facility ranks first in Scotland and third in the United Kingdom.

John Lambert, Charles Fleetwood, John Owen, and Nickolas Lockyer were among Patrick Gillespie's close circle of friends and were influential before, during, and immediately following Cromwell's reign. Charles Fleetwood was married to Cromwell's daughter, Bridget, and was held within the Cromwell family with high esteem. Early in his rule, Cromwell appointed Lambert as Lord Deputy of Ireland. This distinguished group of

Commissioners who were anxious to turn England into an independent democratic republic and commonwealth served the Lord Protector throughout his years in power. Among these distinguished Commissioners were lawyers, theologians, military leaders, and influential scholars. They faithfully assisted Cromwell in his major ecclesiastical, military and political decisions.

John Owen accompanied Cromwell on his Irish campaign where he served as Cromwell's personal Chaplain. For his faithful service and his academic attributes, Cromwell appointed John Owen Vice Chancellor of Oxford University. During his Chancellorship of Oxford, John Owen with a keen interest in his dear friend Patrick Gillespie's "Ark of the Covenant" wrote the Preface to this famous theological text.

Earlier in Cromwell's military campaign against Charles' Royalist, Lambert served as a major general at Dunbar where he defeated Leslie's Covenanters. During his busy Parliamentary service, Lambert wrote Cromwell's "Instrument of Government" which Cromwell's Parliament used in their rule of England. Lambert's "Instrument of Government" is recognized by many as England's first Constitution.

Lambert's Constitution of 1653 established and empowered Cromwell's new Government with legislative power to elect members of Parliament and to establish governing policies. Within these rules for governing was an executive legislature that established Cromwell as the head of state and authorized a fifteen man executive council of state whose members included soldiers, politicians, and religious leaders.

Cromwell's Council of Commissioners issued their Ordinance of Union that abolished among other things all feudal lordships, heritable jurisdictions, military services, and all forfeitures and escheats. From now on, the landlords would have to exchange patronage for wealth. Tenants would not be treated as slaves.

Robert Baille complained cynically about his resentful rival, Patrick Gillespie. He accused Gillespie of wasteful spending. Baille angrily organized a group known as "Resolutioners" to oppose Gillespie.

Robert Baille was jealous of Patrick Gillespie's influence with Cromwell, which included the selection of University officials and ministers. Baille challenged Gillespie's lush lifestyle. In his memoirs, Baille wrote of Gillespie's luxurious rides through Scotland in his royal coach with his legion of twenty Scottish followers riding on their fine steeds .Continuing, Baille ranted how Gillespie preached before Cromwell in his red scarlet cloak.

In Cromwell's absence, during his 1650-51 Scottish and Irish campaigns, factions of the English Parliament engaged in much fighting. When Cromwell returned to London from Ireland, he, without success, tried to unify the Rump Parliament. The Rump legislators ignored the commands of Cromwell and introduced their own bill for a new government. Cromwell became enraged at this Parliament and ordered his musketeers to clear the chambers. The musketeers ran his entire rump parliament out of London.

Cromwell replaced his rump parliament with his bare bones Parliament. This Parliament's legislators had renowned religious credentials, and many were recommended by Patrick Gillespie.

Cromwell ordered his "bare bones" Parliament to draft a permanent Government document using Lambert's constitution and to design a religious settlement. Cromwell discovered many of his Parliament members were associated with the Fifth Monarchrist radical group. This radical group took their name from a prophecy in the Book of Daniel predicting that four monarchies would precede Christ's return to Earth. From fear of these zealots gaining too much control of England, Cromwell dissolved his bare bones Parliament.

Following dissolution of this Parliament, Cromwell established a new constitution known as the "Instrument of Government". Under this document, England knew Cromwell as "Lord Protector". As Lord Protector, Cromwell declared, "My two main objectives are: healing and settling the spiritual and moral reform of England." Parliament wanted to crown Cromwell as King , however, Cromwell refused, remarking, "God's providence has spoken against the office of King". Rather than the customary Westminster Abbey ceremony, England ceremoniously inaugurated Cromwell as "Lord Protector" in a glorious ritual at Westminster Hall where he sat majestically upon King Edward's chair.

Missing from Cromwell's inaugural ceremony, as Lord Protector, were regalia and ceremonial dress. Cromwell insisted that a "Sword of Justice" be the main symbol for his rule. Noticeably missing from Cromwell's head, during the ceremony and throughout his rein, was a crown. Cromwell spoke at length before his Parliament clearly explaining, "My service to you and all of England is as your Lord Protector, and I reign as your constable, or watchman. Future succession to the English throne will not be by heredity".

Cromwell's conquest of Scotland left no lasting bitterness in Scotland. Under Cromwell, Scottish lands were not confiscated. The justices of peace were mostly Scots, with Scotland jointly governed by Cromwell's military and the Scottish Council of State.

Unlike any other European ruler, Cromwell rose as a private citizen and heroically gained, with his devoted military of Roundheads, the rule of a great European nation. Cromwell changed England's ancient frame of Government with his Parliament and written constitution.

Following his bare bones Parliament, Cromwell introduced a form of Government based on a balance of power with duties contained in a reformed single chamber of Parliament. Governance was by a new system of representatives, an elected council, and the executive Lord Protector, Cromwell.

Sadly, Cromwell was many years ahead of England's willingness to accept Parliamentary rule. Queen Elizabeth's Parliamentary, Puritan, rule was somewhat more successful. Many scholars indicate her success was due to her political savvy and judicious Privy Council, consisting of faithful members like William Cecil and Sir Francis Walsingham. They were diplomatic politicians who interfaced effectively with the commoners as well as members of Parliament.

Cromwell died in 1658 from a bout with malaria without achieving his dream of Parliamentary-Constitutional rule for Great Britain. England honored Cromwell's death with an enormous burial ceremony held at Westminster Abbey. Gillespie and his close friends; especially Lambert, vigorously opposed any return to power to Charles II.

General Monck, a Presbyterian, who earlier had faithfully signed Scotland's Covenant, was behind the scenes and began negotiating with Parliament and Charles to restore the monarchy.

Following Cromwell's death, affairs in Britain had become chaotic as the country staggered toward anarchy. Three independent English Armies, the Navy, the Rump Parliament, the Royalists, and a number of religious factions all competed for power. The confused affairs of England cried out for an experienced and bold leader to take charge of the country.

Lambert led a legion of Parliament troops to oppose Charles' supporters led by Monck. In total surprise, Lambert's troops were persuaded that the restoration of Charles II to the throne would benefit the nation and Lambert's troops faded away. They joined Monck's army and left Lambert without an army. Monck, without any bloodshed, marched to London and convinced Parliament to join his campaign to restore Charles II to England's throne.

With the return of King Charles from hiding in France, the freedom-loving Covenanters were in for a major and ruthless turn of events. King Charles betrayed many of the Covenanter Engagers who so faithfully protected him from capture by Cromwell.

Had the Covenanters remained united throughout Cromwell's Protectorate, England's destiny would have been much brighter. The horrific persecutions administered for over a quarter century by the wicked Stuart Kings upon the humble Covenanters, during the Crown's murderous "killing fields", probably would not have occurred under a united Covenanter front.

Unfortunately, upon the death of Cromwell, Britain's political and military affairs became near anarchy, which led to destruction of the Constitutional Parliamentary efforts of Cromwell. Cromwell's Puritan reign had rid Britain of "Kingly Rights" and had eliminated the monarch and House of Lords. Through Cromwell's Constitution and Council of State justice was administered throughout Britain, which provided liberties for the common man.

Britain's hectic and unruly chaos was driven by a number of factions; several armies, the Parliament, the contending Royalists and a host of religious divisions wherein each vied to control national affairs.

With Charles' return to the throne the faithful Presbyterians, who fought for him so valiantly, were in for a rude awakening and horrific surprise. Lurking in the shadows of evil to support Charles with his forthcoming vindictive cruelties was his wicked brother James II. The latter was ready to inflict enormous atrocities on Scotland's heroic Covenanters as defenders of freedom and liberty for the common man.

Chapter 7
King Charles II's Restoration of His "Kingly Rights"e.g. Monarchy and Persecution of the Covenanters

In 1660 after Cromwell's death, General Monck paved the way for the return of Charles II to the English throne. During much confusion and indecisiveness of England's Parliament and militia, General Monck slid over to Charles' Royalist camp to lead his Royalists in the defeat of the remnants of Cromwell's Protectorate.

Led by Monck, Charles' supporters escorted him to London to take the crown. In the interim, Charles' many Anglican and Catholic friends provided much support for his takeover of England.

Many Engagers, also, continued to support Charles II. Charles deceitfully agreed that if the Presbyterians helped him to regain his throne, he would guarantee Presbyterian worship and freedom of religion. Instead, after regaining the throne, Charles jailed the freedom loving Puritans and drove them from their churches.

King Charles II maliciously destroyed the cherished Scottish Covenant and Solemn League documents. He began persecuting his former Scotch Presbyterian allies. King Charles dug up Cromwell's corpse from his honored burial place in Westminster Abbey and hideously hanged his skeleton by chains in the Abbey Courtyard in total mockery of Cromwell's rule.

The horrific treatment inflicted by King Charles II on Presbyterian families defied imagination. Throughout Scotland, the floodgates of vengeful cruelty opened. Little villages of humble Puritan worshippers ,from moor to glen, suffered beyond imagination.

King Charles appointed Robert Baille, who earlier supported the Engagers in their support of Charles at the battle of Dunbar, to replace Patrick Gillespie as Principal of

Glasgow University. Despite serving in the 1640's with Patrick Gillespie's brother George in the Westminster Assembly, Baille much disliked Patrick. Baille's animosity toward Patrick stemmed in part from his jealously of the Gillespie family's close friendship with Cromwell.

King Charles imprisoned Samuel Rutherford, Gillespie's dearest friend, and Scotland's renowned theologian. King Charles immediately burned all copies found of Rutherford's famous book, "Lex Rex," and all of George Gillespie's famous theological writings. Ironically, Rutherford robbed King Charles of his opportunity to hold a mock trial when the theologian died in prison before Charles could arrange his beheading. Rutherford died with the joyful exclamation, "Glory Shineth in Immanuel's Land".

King Charles vengefully demanded that Archbishop Sharp order his hangman to break George Gillespie's Kirkcaldy Kirk tombstone and church memorial. The Crown issued authority and Commissions to the British noblemen and military officers of Scotland to convict all the opposing Presbyterian inhabitants. Many Covenanters over fourteen years of age were executed by the King's rogues. Throughout Scotland roving Anglican scoundrels burned Covenanter homes or seized their property. King Charles imposed an oath of adjuration throughout the countryside to which many faithful Covenanters refused to comply. Upon their refusal, Charles' cruel thugs merrily cut off their ears or other extremities and banished many from England as slaves.

During these murderous times of the Stuart Kings, the English Puritans struggled desperately to rid England of Charles II, his cruel brother James Duke of York and their cruel operatives.

King Charles II and his sadist brother James declared the entire South of Scotland as a hunting field to inflict terror and torture. King Charles' equestrians and their vicious hunting dogs ran down many Presbyterian men and women. Fortunately, the King's vicious hunters usually spared those under the age of fourteen. King Charles' avengers captured and imprisoned many thousands of helpless freedom-loving villagers. Many died from the hideous tortures ordered by King Charles and when James II became King these tortures increased. A favorite sport that James' rogues used to murder Covenanters was to drag their bound captives to the beach at low tide where they were staked. Many freedom-loving Puritans died a slow cruel death as the powerful tides of the North Sea rose slowly over their heads. Another favorite drowning site was Solway Firth, an arm of the Irish Sea that forms part of the border between England and Scotland.

(**"King James II's Solway Firth Drownings i.e.
Margaret Wilson- Terrifyingly the tide slowly rose)**
During his exile in France, Charles II boldly seized
the opportunity to reward his supporters with large grants
of land in Virginia and other American colonies. Charles
granted the entire Northern neck of Virginia, the land
between the Rappahannock and Potomac Rivers, to friends
of his monarchy. He rewarded Lord Culpepper and six
other supporters with Virginia land grants. Shortly after
returning from France, Charles, to ensure the continued
support of his Anglican Royalists, continued, per whim, to

grant America's lands as incentives. In 1663 Charles bribed eight of his faithful, Anglican Royalists, known as Lord Proprietors, with vast land grants in the Carolinas. These Proprietors issued quit-rents to the immigrant settlers to pay for their proprietary local government. These corrupted quit-rents also supported the lavish spending of the King's governor Tryon.

McCulloch's corrupt quit-rent practices, supported by Governor Tryon, horribly affected the well-being of the freedom-loving Scots-Irish in the Carolinas, especially Mecklenburg and Alamance County farmers.

Among the Lord Proprietors who were induced to support King Charles was General Monck. To ensure Monck's support, Charles generously appointed him as Lord Albemarle. As Lord Albemarle, Monck received thousands of acres from Charles II along Carolina's coastline. The Albemarle Sound carries the Lord Albemarle name as a General Monck remembrance.

Meanwhile, in April 1673, a Privy Council sentenced Minister Robert Gillespie, the son of the renowned theologian George Gillespie and the Great Grandfather of Duplin County's James Gillespie to prison on Bass Rock. King Charles imprisoned Minister Gillespie for holding, without the Crown's prior approval, a house conventicle in Falkland to preach the Presbyterian faith.

The fortress of Bass Rock is an insular trap rock at the mouth of the Firth of Forth, one mile off North Berwick. The Rock is in a circular form of one mile circumference and rises majestically out of the sea to a height of over 300 feet. In the 1670's, King Charles II used Bass Rock as a notorious prison. Charles locked and tortured many famous religious and political prisoners on Bass Rock, including Robert Erskine a renowned Scottish political figure.

"Bass Rock King Charles II's famous prison site for Covenanters"

Robert Gillespie suffered horribly in his prison vault. The size of his cell was 55 feet by 15 feet, with 12-foot high walls. Two tiny cell-vault windows, secured by crowbars, served for feeding and watering. The vault's window provided little ventilation for Robert to breath. Repulsive jailers used wrist size notches, cut in the wall above Robert's reach, to suspend him for hours by his hands. When the grisly jailer received enough cruel gratification, he, with hideous pleasure, leisurely lowered Robert to the floor. His space to sit or sleep was incredibly cramped and filled with human waste. Many of Gillespie's cell mates died on top of one another.

Reverend Robert Gillespie miraculously survived imprisonment in his vastly undersized vault, ankle deep with human filth. His space, to sit or sleep, was cramped and filled with human waste. Many of Gillespies' cellmates died on top of one another.

Through the Grace of God and by Robert's promising to observe the King's indulgence rules imposed on the Scottish ministers, King Charles released Gillespie from Bass Rock. Through his mother's intensive nurturing, over several years, Robert regained his health. As he promised the King to gain his freedom, Minister Gillespie preached at Fife Shire and many other Kirks, carefully observing the King's requirements.

Gillespie, as a leading Scottish minister, was commanded by King Charles to supervise his indulgence crusade. Under the King's orders, the Scottish ministers could only preach when licensed by King Charles. The King forced strict regulations upon the ministers and required that they must minister as per the Crown's rules. In fear of terrible repercussions, Presbyterian ministers carefully preached and praised the Crown as King Charles demanded. They were careful to praise and never criticize King Charles.

To maintain harmony with the Crown and preserve the Presbyterian faith, Robert Gillespie reluctantly, against his beliefs, led the meetings of ministers in the country side and around the Fife. He advised his fellow ministers how best to adhere to the King's Indulgences so as to deter the Presbyterian clergy's torture and imprisonment.

The Puritans referred to Richard Cameron as the "Lion of the Covenanters." In August of 1678, he returned from his safe haven in Rotterdam. Maurice Grant's book entitled "The Lion of the Covenanters" depicts Cameron's life and his brave vehement preaching against the many corruptions of the Stuart Kings.

Without hesitation, Cameron bravely preached the Presbyterian liturgy throughout Northeast Scotland. He ignored King Charles' regulations that rigidly controlled and monitored Scotland's ecclesiastical affairs. Cameron was disciplined at several meetings of Scottish ministers, led by Robert Gillespie, for not adhering to the King's regulations. Unfortunately, Richard Cameron ignored the wise advice of Gillespie and other Covenanter ministers.

The ministers, all too well, knew that to escape the cruel tortures of Charles II they must abide by his unjust religious decrees.

Soon Andrew Bruce of Earlshall, one of King Charles' assassins, killed Cameron. Several years earlier, the Bruce family had been friends of the Cameron family. Bruce and his authoritarian followers gruesomely beheaded Cameron and crammed his head into a burlap sack. These rogues carried Cameron's skull around the countryside for several weeks as they bragged about their murderous deed.

----In 1816, Walter Scott wrote his famous love novel "Old Mortality" about a Covenanter who sought the love of a Royalist Lady Bellandale. Within Scott's novel is a vivid description of the violent skirmishes between Charles' Royalists and the destitute and downtrodden Presbyterians in their determined efforts to preserve their religious faith. Over 270 Presbyterian ministers refused to take Charles' oath of allegiance and accept his religious indulgency regulations. They refused to submit their ministry to Episcopalian Bishops. These ministers bravely led their parishioners in worship throughout many locations in the Scottish countryside. Charles, continually, sent out his troops to prevent these faithful worshipers from holding their peaceful prayer meetings.

Scott's novel described the horrific persecution of the Presbyterian Covenanters through an old and faithful Covenanter in his dying days. The humble Covenanter, near death, respectfully staggered about the countryside telling his horrendous story about the murderous deeds of King Charles II and his brother James' many inflictions upon his fellow parishioners. The old, devoted, Covenanter struggled so relentlessly to restore the many Covenanter tombstones in the Dunnator Kirk graveyard. King James' cruel militia had massacred these brave Covenanters at Bothwell Bridge on the River Clyde. Following the atrocious Bothwell Bridge murders, many of these pitiful dying Presbyterians found refuge in Duchess Anne's Hamilton Palace between the town of Hamilton and Clyde.

Fortunately for the Covenanters and especially for the Gillespies, the overthrow of King James by King William of Orange ended the Stuart King's hunting fields of terror.

In the early 1700's, the Glasgow Presbytery licensed Robert's son, George, to become a Presbyterian minister. In 1712, George Gillespie emigrated to Boston through the support and recommendations provided by Cotton Mather that were approved by the Glasgow Presbytery through Dr. Sterling, the Principal of Glasgow University. Earlier in 1710, George Gillespie and Cotton Mather were classmates at Glasgow University where Dr. Sterling awarded their Doctorates of Divinity.

George Gillespie first preached at a small Boston parish. After a year of ministering in Boston, George Gillespie in 1714 with Cotton Mather's support obtained his own ministry in Woodridge, New Jersey.

Following a year of ministry in Woodridge, George Gillespie, supported by the Glasgow Presbytery, became the first appointed minister of Newark Delaware's, New Castle County's Christiana Presbyterian log church. Gillespie wrote several widely read theological manuscripts. One document was entitled, "A Treatise against Deist and Freethinkers." George Gillespie served as minister of the Christiana Presbyteria until his death in 1760. Minister Gillespie and his two sons are buried in the Christiana Church cemetery, as well as many revolutionary war soldiers.

In the early 1700's, Cotton Mather founded a number of small classical schools in the Boston countryside. During this period, Mather assisted his father in the founding of what became Yale University. These early 1700 religious and educational efforts by Cotton

Mather and his father, along with other Presbyterian ministers with their many log churches, provided a foundation for William Tennent and Jonathan Edwards to begin their revival crusade across America. During the 1720's, the stormy preaching of Edwards and Tennant became known as America's "Great Awakening". These religious revivals of America's "Great Awakening" provided important social and political influences in direct opposition to those of England's Anglican Church. Throughout colonial America, the many Presbyterian revivals provided a stepping-stone and spirit for the colonies' upcoming revolution for freedom from the English Crown.

These early pioneering evangelistic and educational efforts by Mather, Tennant, Jonathan Edwards and other Presbyterian ministers provided a foundation for America's first Universities, i.e. Harvard, William and Mary, Yale and Princeton. Princeton provided a stepping stone for America's first public University, the University of North Carolina (UNC). Most of UNC's first professors were graduates of Princeton, including Professors James Smiley Gillespie and James Harris. These Universities, essentially Presbyterian pioneering seminaries, played a crucial role in gaining freedom from England through their steadfast teachings of political and religious philosophy based on "liberty of conscience". Their teachings conditioned the minds of colonial America for rebellion against the Crown's "Kingly Rights".

Charles II, prior to his death in 1685, announced James II, his cruel brother, was to succeed him on the throne. Upon Charles' death, many of Charles' close friends believed that James had poisoned him.

Upon being crowned King of England, in February 1685, James II immediately began filling parliament with all of his Catholic friends. King James committed many wicked acts in the presence of his own young daughters

Mary and Anne. They witnessed with horror the many atrocities of their father and his close circle of papist and corrupt friends. In their teen-age years, they made a pact that they would betray their father and remove him from the English throne.

Having tolerated her father's cruelties as long as she could, Princess Mary desperately sought a means of escape. The Princess, at her first opportunity, secretly sailed to Holland where she married Prince William of Orange. The couple, with their many Dutch supporters, began planning and gathering support to remove their father, James, from the throne. Meanwhile, Princess Anne made her own plans, in 1683, and secretly married Prince George of Denmark.

During this time, King James announced the birth of a son, which everyone doubted was his. Princess Anne had proof her father smuggled a new born son into his wife's bed chamber. James named the newborn baby boy, he announced as his son, James Francis Edward Stuart.

In the early 1700's, England's Jacobites supported James Francis, whom they named the "Old Pretender" in hopes the Catholic backed Stuarts would regain the throne. Later in the 1740's, England's Jacobites supported James Francis Edward Stuart's son, whom they called "Bonnie Prince Charlie", in their last futile attempt to regain the crown for the Stuart's.

Meanwhile King James' rule, with his parliamentary Catholic friends, became more and more intolerable for the country's many Puritans.

Princess Anne enthusiastically aided her sister Mary and husband Prince William with their secretive plans to overthrow their father King James. In November 1688, the Dutch troops of William of Orange invaded England. Princess Anne, to escape the uprising, became exiled in Holland. She wrote her brother-in-law, William, wishing him well in his invasion to rid England of her father's brutal and wicked rule. Princess Anne's husband,

George, left with James' army. During the confusion of the uprising he quickly changed over to King William's camp. William landed his troops and began his attack on London. William's militia faced little resistance when many of James' officers refused to take orders to attack William's troops. Frustrated, King James and his troops were quickly overpowered and James quietly slipped away from the melee. He escaped to his Catholic friends in France. Facing little resistance, William rode triumphantly into London and heroically claimed the throne to begin his Glorious Revolution.

Part III – King William's Glorious Revolution and Queen Anne's Reign (1688-1714)

During the years of the Glorious Revolution, Great Britain overthrew the barbaric King James II. The Puritans fought valiantly to break King James' siege of the city of Derry, in Ulster, Ireland. Their victory at the Battle of the Boyne, Ulster ensured victory for King William's, Anglican-Protestant Army over King James' Irish and French Catholic soldiers.

Under the leadership of Queen Mary and King William, Britain gained a "Bill of Rights" ensuring civil liberties. Under Queen Anne's reign, parliament passed the "Act of Union" which combined Scotland, Ireland, and England to establish the United Kingdom. Queen Anne's United Kingdom, through the military leadership of Lord Marlborough, defeated Spain and France. Marlborough neutralized a powerful European Catholic monarch that favored the Jacobites. Without Marlborough's stunning victories, Catholics would probably have returned to rule England.

Again, the tides turned against the faithful Protestant Scots-Irish when Queen Anne, in 1703, encouraged by her aristocratic Anglican friends instituted her "Test Acts". This legislation greatly restricted the freedom of the Presbyterians and removed their rights to hold any Crown (Government) position.

Chapter 8
The Glorious Revolution

Following Charles II's return to the throne, many Scots fled the terrors of the Stuarts by rowing across the twenty mile Northern Irish Sea to Ulster Ireland. The frequent passage of Scots and Irish back and forth between Ulster and Scotland was similar to a scheduled ferry.

In late 1687, the three sons of Reverend Robert Gillespie, David, John and James, along with countless other Presbyterians in Scotland, feared for their lives. They escaped Scotland and the persecution inflicted on Scotland's Covenanters by King James during his killing fields of torture. They joined their many Scottish Presbyterian friends in Ulster. The three Gillespie brothers arrived in Ulster eager to support King William's overthrow of King James II, hopefully, the last of the Stuart Kings.

The Puritans, Presbyterians and Anglicans alike, frantically ran from James' Catholic troops to Londonderry to escape the murderous wrath of James. James in his brutal attack on non-Catholic sections of Ireland instilled terror on all freedom loving Protestants throughout the Irish countryside.

In 1689, terror struck the many Protestants as they frantically sought refuge from King James' cruelties and his Catholic allies. Fortunately, the garrisons in the city of Londonderry and the town of Inniskillin opened their gates to provide refuge for the many endangered Presbyterians and Anglicans who were fleeing from the onslaught of James' Irish Catholic and French soldiers.

King James, after he escaped to France from William of Orange's assault, sought out the assistance of French Catholic soldiers and sailed back to Dublin with his military supporters in an attempt to regain the English Crown. James' military strategy, using his preponderant Catholic support in Ireland, was first to annihilate the Irish

Protestants. He next crossed the Irish Sea to join his Catholic sympathizers in Scotland and establish a Scottish stronghold. The final stage of James' grand plan to regain the throne was an assault on London and the capture of England.

A number of Gillespie families, along with almost six thousand other brave Protestants, sought refuge from the terrors of King James inside the gates of Londonderry. The besieged decided not to open the gates to James. James, mounted on his fine steed, waited outside Derry's walls like a hungry wolf ready to devour his trapped prey.

"DERRY WALLS - CASTLE GATE"

Impatiently waiting outside the gates, James soon left. He ordered his Catholic troops to attack Derry on April 18, 1689. Derry was the last remaining Protestant stronghold in Ireland. These brave Protestants trapped inside Derry, held out against the Papist bombardment of their city walls. They miraculously detained James' French and Irish troops in Ireland and prevented a supply of soldiers and supplies for James' other battles across Ireland. Their brave holdout in their starving siege for over three long months greatly assisted King William's victory at the Battle of the Boyne.

These besieged Protestants prayed that their scant store of grain would be sufficient until King William's soldiers could rescue them. Early in the siege, James' Catholic soldiers brought several hundred naked and starving Protestant prisoners from Inniskillin and many captives from around the Irish countryside to the walls of Derry. The Papist troops announced to their trapped Protestant prey inside the walls, "Your captive Protestant friends and relatives held outside these walls will be murdered if you keep the gates closed." Inside the brave fugitives yelled, "We won't open the gates!" Courageously they kept the gates barred shut. Outside, the many brave, bleeding captives loudly screamed, "For the sake of King Billy, don't open the gates." James' cruel Catholics furiously slaughtered their helpless captives. Inside, the many trapped Presbyterians stoically refused to open the gates. Soon, they ate all their food and they were left in dire circumstances. Londonderry's besieged inhabitants had to eat cats, dogs, horses, and dead humans.

On July 31, 1689, after nearly three months, the ships Mount Joy and Phoenix, sent by William and Mary arrived. Miraculously the two ships broke through the river blockades and rescued Derry's starving captives. At the time of rescue, the only food remaining were several rib-boney starved horses and a small portion of meal. Half of the seven thousand Protestants, trapped behind city walls died of starvation.

The suffering and terrors of Londonderry's besieged were great. The Puritan captives considered their sacrifice was honorable and worthy since the long detainment of the cruel papists greatly assisted in the defeat of King James. Many Protestants in Ireland's countryside suffered equally or greater than the captives of Derry.

On July 1, 1689, during the horrific terrors of Londonderry's besieged, the decisive battle between King James II and King William of Orange was fought. The main battle raged over the control of a ford on the Boyne River near the Hamlet of Old Bridge.

David Gillespie, son of Minister Robert Gillespie, fought furiously across the River Boyne with the Dutch Blue Guards and assisted in the capture of the Village of Oldbridge. Gillespie and the Blue Guards secured the village and held off King James II's Jacobite cavalry attacks. Under the vicious attacks of the Dutch Blue Guards the Jacobites retreated and lost the Battle of Boyne.

His long sword, that helped swing the Scots- Irish again to "**FREEDOM**", holds many precious memories. Today David's heroic efforts at the Boyne River support tales of bravery told by his many descendants in the County of Monaghan, Ireland and across America.

Following the Londonderry siege, the many Presbyterians who braved their starving entrapment were greatly angered to learn that the Anglican elite had claimed most of the credit for the Puritan's stand behind Londonderry's walls. During the years following the Glorious Revolution, the many disputes among the Presbyterians and the Anglicans convinced Ulster's Scottish Presbyterians that Ireland's Catholic -Anglican noxious society was not their desired homeland.

Throughout his terrifying reign, King James II had imposed hardships and suffering on the faithful freedom loving Scots- Irish Protestants.

(Up to and through England's Glorious Revolution, John Locke, England's famous empiricist, published a number of political and religious writings. His renowned political theory, " All human nature is characterized by reason and tolerance, and all people are equal and independent, and everyone has a right to pursue life, health, and liberty" greatly supported freedom and liberties during England's Glorious Revolution. Thomas Jefferson in America's Declaration of Independence borrowed Locke's famous political philosophy, "the unalienable rights to pursue Life, Liberty, and Happiness are self-evident".)

Early in King William and Queen Mary's reign the Scots-Irish Presbyterians supported by their steadfast Whig supporters in Parliament, were instrumental in Parliament's ratifying England's "Bill of Rights". These "Bill of Rights" established the rights of subjects and residents in England under a constitutional monarchy for subjects. England's Bill of Rights constitutionally required the King to obtain Parliament's permission before the Crown could legally act, such as in taxing citizens. Parliament and the populace received the following civil and political rights:

*Freedom of religion
*Freedom from Royal interference with the law
*Freedom from Royal taxes unless approved by Parliament
*Freedom to petition the monarch
*Parliament's approval of the use of the Army against the populace *Freedom for Protestants to bear arms in their own defense
*Freedom of speech and debates in Parliament without impeachment or questioned in any court out of Parliament.

In 1701 their "Act of Settlement" and their "Claim

of Right Act" established Parliaments' rights and reduced the powers of the King. This legislation established constitutional rule with penal laws. The "Bill of Rights" greatly supported the settlement of political and religious turmoil in England, Scotland, and Ireland.

After enduring many long years of torture and persecution, the Scots-Irish Presbyterians, under King William, finally obtained basic human rights and "freedom of worship".

Less than a century later Scots-Irish emigrants, mostly Presbyterians, insisted upon a "Bill Of Rights" as the first ten amendments to the new nation's Constitution. They were patterned after England's "Bill of Rights". George Mason drafted such a "Bill of Rights" and lobbied long and hard for acceptance by the Philadelphia Constitutional Assembly. The Federal assembly introduced the new nation's Constitution without a "Bill of Rights" to the individual State's Constitutional Convention of delegates for ratification. Several states, greatly influenced by the loud outcry of the Scots-Irish, refused ratification. These principled Scots-Irishmen were protectors of the rights of common man. They insisted upon a "Bill of Rights" before they would consider ratification of the U. S. Constitution.

In the 1690's, David Gillespie received Ulster land grants from King William for his service during the Battle of Boyne. He used these land grants to raise flax. The Gillespie family spun the fiber's strands into Irish linen. They grounded the flax seed into meal which they mixed in oatmeal and flour to make delicious breads with a nutty flavor. Also from flax seed, they made linseed oil, as well as medicine.

The Gillespie's and other Scots-Irish families sold their fine quality Irish linen and lace in the Belfast market. Belfast provided Ulster with an excellent sheltered seaport for their thriving linens-woolen trade. The woolen and linen industry of the Scots-Irish brought much prosperity to Northern Ireland. The fine quality of Belfast linen, however, undermined the English woolen market in direct competition with the finer Irish linen. In turn, the English lost much of their market.

To protect their fabric market, the English Parliament passed the 1699 "Woolens Act", which blocked the Scots-Irish from marketing their fabrics. Under their Woolens Act, England controlled the price of Ulster's linen. Sale of Irish linen was restricted to only England and Wales, which allowed England's strict control over the price and sale of Irish linen goods. The Woolens Act severely crippled the Ulster linen industry.

To add further misery, the English landlords introduced rack- rents (under the rack- rent the landlord could exert his power to charge excessive rent, to confiscate wages and to evict tenants) on the rich fertile Scots-Irish farmlands given by King William to the Protestant Scots for their bravery in defeating King James II. During this time of abusive and crooked rack-renting, landlord property owners raised the rent of their impoverished tenants to incredibly high and un-payable prices.

In the early 1700's, David Gillespie Sr. married a Miss Borthick. Their first child was a son, David Junior. The Gillespie family lived on their farm in Shantine and raised flax from which they made the finest of linen drapery. In 1724 David Junior married a Miss Brison of Shantine and they raised five children: Jane, Archibald, Borthick, David III and James. Born in 1746, James was the youngest of David Gillespie's children. David Gillespie Jr. due to the harsh living conditions sought a brighter future for his sons.

Chapter 9
Reign of Queen Anne

Sadly, the Gillespies and other Presbyterians lost a true friend when King William died from a riding accident in 1702. William's favorite warhorse Sorrell tripped in a ground-hog hole and seriously injured King William. The King died within a few days from his riding accident. Queen Mary, William's beloved wife, died earlier of smallpox in 1694.

Queen Anne became Queen of England after William's death. Under Queen Anne's reign, the Stuart Kings' violence of the 17th century was over but not forgotten. Queen Anne inspired the English to begin a new century, the 18th, with renewed stability and prosperity. In 1707, Queen Anne's Act of Union united England, Scotland and Ireland forming the Kingdom of Great Britain.

Corruptly persuaded by her aristocratic Anglican followers, Queen Anne in 1703 forced her cruel Anglican "Test Acts" upon all Puritans and Catholics. These Test Acts severely limited their freedom. The humble Scots-Irishmen, who had fought so courageously in King William's Glorious Revolution in the defeat of King James and his evil Papist regime, were totally forsaken. Queen Anne's Test Acts" prohibited the Presbyterians and all religious sects, other than Anglican, from holding public office, prevented their clergy from performing marriage ceremonies as well as burial services, and imposed many other cruel restrictions to religious freedom. These Test Acts barred Presbyterians and Catholics alike from their government positions which created total chaos throughout Ulster.

Again, the Presbyterian Scots-Irish were ignored and forgotten for their heroic efforts in defeating the forces of King James II. Sadly, the "tides of freedom" had ebbed and once again turned against these freedom-loving Scots-

Irish. They soon began dreaming and planning to migrate to America to seek their religious and political freedom.

During most of Queen Anne's reign Great Britain fought the War of Spanish succession. Under the brilliant military leadership of the Duke of Marlborough, Britain, Holland, Portugal, and the Holy Roman Empire fought France and Spain to prevent the French and Spaniards from forming a unified European Catholic monarchy. The Duke of Marlborough, with his crushing victory at the battle of Blenheim, forced the treaties of Utrecht in 1713 and Rastatt in 1714 preventing a controlling Catholic European monarchy from materializing. Obviously, Queen Anne's Treaties helped control the Jacobite's ambitions for regaining the British Crown.

In 1707 more than a half century after Cromwell's valiant attempt to provide England with a Parliamentary government and Constitution, Queen Anne's "Acts of Union" provided a Parliament for Great Britain. However, in practice the Parliament formed was a continuation of the English Parliament that allowed the addition of Scottish members. England's legislative authority had three separate elements, the Monarch, the House of Lords, and the House of Commons. English citizens elected members of the House of Commons and Parliament selected the House of Lords.

England continued with their "Kingly Rights Principles" and structured the House of Lords to be superior to that of the House of Commons, both in theory and in practice. Fortunately, in the early 20th century, out of demand from English citizens, the House of Commons obtained supremacy over the House of Lords whose selected members consisted of ruling class landlords and Anglican bishops. The power of the House of Lords is, to some extent, dominated by the patronage and influence of English nobility. Over the 18th Century, the King struggled to maintain royal supremacy and control over Parliament.

Although the "Act of Union" did not provide Scotland with the most favorable Parliamentary rule, Scotland, fortunately, underwent an era of technological enlightenment. During the 18th century, Scotland was the world's intellectual center supported by their four renowned universities: Glasgow, Edinburgh, St. Andrews and Aberdeen.

Scotland's scientific and intellectual accomplishments were the envy of the world. Scotland produced many renowned scholars and scientists, including: Robert Burns as a poet, David Hume as a Philosopher, James Watt as an inventor of the steam engine, and Joseph Priestly as the discoverer of oxygen. Robert Burns emigrated to America and wrote many poems for America's freedom, including a special "ode" to General Washington. Scotland proudly published its Encyclopedia Britannica to demonstrate to the world its many amazing achievements.

Anne was the last of the Stuart family to reign. Graciously, she attempted to put her Stuart family's terrible persecution of the Presbyterian Covenanters behind. However, her "Test Acts" encouraged and orchestrated by her Anglican friends once again renewed the hatred between the Presbyterians and Anglicans.

All of Queen Anne's children died at an early age and Anne had no heir for the throne. Searching in 1714 for a Protestant, Queen Anne finally selected a distant cousin George, from Germany's "House of Hanover," to be her heir to England's throne. King George I was about 50th in line for the throne; however as Queen Anne desired she ensured her successor for England's throne was a Protestant.

During the 17th century battles between the Presbyterian Covenanters and the Stuart Papist regimes the Whig and Tory political parties, that exist today, were organized. The Presbyterian political cause, led by

Rutherford, Gillespie, Henderson and other great Scottish theologians in the 1630-40's against the Royalists became known as the Whig Party. Many referred to the Whigs as Presbyterian guerilla fighters. King James' supporters, mostly Papists, in the 1670-80's, began the Tory political party often referred to as the King supported "Irish bandits." For over three centuries, the Whig and Tory parties have remained the mainstays of Britain's two party system.

Part IV- Jacobites Fail to Restore the Stuart Monarch (1715-1747)
Chapter 10
Jacobite Rebellions

The Catholic supported Jacobites (Latin for James) were livid over Queen Anne's selection of George a German-speaking Protestant from the House of Hanover as King of England. Over the next half century, the Catholics plotted, with many schemes, to restore the Stuart family to the throne.

During the early 1700's, the Scottish Jacobites who lived in Scotland's northern highlands were known as "highlanders". Mostly sheep and cattle herders, these highlanders lived in closely knitted village clans and worked as tenants for the rich landlord barons.

The Scottish Hanoverian supporters, typically rich land barons, resided in southern Scotland and controlled the wealth of Scotland. They rented their large plantations to the Jacobite highlanders and increased their wealth by shrewd management of their linen factories and large flax plantations.

As portrayed by the movie "Rob Roy", the Hanoverian land barons mistreated "Rob" Roy McGregor, a Jacobite cattle thief. Rob Roy, idolized by the Jacobite Highlanders as a "Robin Hood", collected ransoms from the rich land barons for protection of their huge cattle herds. He generously distributed his ransoms to the poor downtrodden highlanders. Rob Roy collected his cattle throughout the Scottish countryside and herded his cattle to Craiff, Scotland's large central market. In Craiff he sold his huge herds of stolen cattle.

In 1715 James Stuart , who everyone doubted was the son of King James II, was referred to as the "old pretender". "The old pretender" led a Jacobite rebellion to take the throne which the Protestant supported Crown easily squelched. Luckily, the old Pretender escaped to his

Catholic friends in France.

Again, in the early 1740's, the Jacobites were optimistic that the Stuart family would gain the throne with the oncoming of **Bonnie Prince Charlie** the son of the "old pretender". The Jacobites were much encouraged by Prince Charlie's appearance on the battlefield and provided support for him when he landed on the coast of Scotland. Upon arrival, he organized a small army of patriotic highlanders. The Jacobites, backed by other Catholics, attacked the protestant Hanoverians hoping to win the throne. The Jacobites captured Edinburgh and crossed into Derby England. To the surprise and disappointment of the Jacobites, England failed to support the Catholic's quest for the throne.

Meanwhile, Prince Charlie's army advised the Prince to relax over the winter. Restless, Prince Charlie commanded his troops and led the Jacobite cause against the Protestants and was defeated at the "Moor of Culloden" in April 1746.

Following the Jacobite loss at Culloden, one of King George II's three sons, William Augustus, proceeded to destroy most of the clan system in the northern highlands. He brutally killed many Catholic highlanders which earned him the nick-name "butcher".

In 1746, after the Battle of Culloden, Bonnie Prince Charlie sought refuge in Scotland's Hebrides Islands. Ironically, Flora McDonald a Presbyterian was secretly sympathetic to Prince Charlie. Flora obtained a pass from a family member for herself, her rowing crew, and her royal passenger who was disguised as an Irish house cleaner. Flora and her royal passenger rowed undetected to the mainland. When Flora reached the Isle of Skye, she secretly obtained permission to take the prince to the Isle of Ramsey. The boatmen's gossip led Scottish authorities to Flora McDonald. The authorities accused her of aiding the Prince's escape. King George arrested Flora and imprisoned her in the tower of London. In 1747 Flora gained her freedom under England's "Act of Indemnity".

King George II, during this period, replaced his father, King George I, and ruled until his death in 1760.

Part V- America's Presbyterian Rebellion (1740-1781)

(Scots-Irish migration to America and Presbyterian's Rebellion against Cornwallis in the Carolina Backcountry Drives the British Army to Meet Their Demise at Yorktown.)

During the American Revolution, the Gillespies risked life and property to ensure that colonials gained the freedom and liberties which the English Crown had denied them for many years through appointed colonial governors and taxation without representation. Seeking Freedom for the common man, Congressman James Gillespie and other Scots-Irish legislators insisted that the "Bill of Rights" be the first ten amendments to the U. S. Constitution. These protections against abuse by the new federal government would protect from any continuation of fiat by a King or other despot.

This "Quest for Freedom" confirms the argument that Scots-Irish Presbyterians emigrated to America and continued to curb the English Crown's abuse of central power. They were instrumental in winning America's freedom from the world's most dominant military power, the English Empire. The courageous Scots-Irish defeated British General Cornwallis in Carolina's backcountry in the battles of King's Mountain, Cow Pens, and Guilford Courthouse. These victories led to Cornwallis' entrapment at Yorktown that won the Revolutionary War.

Chapter 11
David Gillespie's Three Young Sons Sail to America

Following King George's defeat of Bonnie Prince Charlie in 1746, increased numbers of Scots-Irish, especially the many sympathizers of the Jacobites in their lost battles to regain the English Crown for the Stuarts, migrated to the Carolinas to escape persecution from Queen Anne's Test Acts and a terrible famine.

Among the many Scots-Irish seeking relief from the terrible Ulster famine, the religious persecutions of Queen Anne's Test Acts and the uprisings of the Ulster landlords were David Gillespie's three young sons James, Archibald, and Borthick. David Gillespie sought an improved life for his sons from continued Ulster hardships. Having suffered through many years of Anglican religious discrimination in Ulster, the young Gillespie lads, similar to thousands of other Scots-Irish, sought relief from the Crown's unfair, and especially cruel, political and religious controls. Additionally, the harsh times created by Ulster's latest famine had been especially difficult on the Gillespies as well as other families of Ulster.

In the spring of 1751, the three young Gillespie brothers were placed on board a squat frigate loaded with other Scots-Irish by their father, David Gillespie Junior. Prior to departing from Belfast, David Gillespie gave the ship's Captain a special dispatch with orders to deliver his young sons to friends waiting anxiously for their arrival in New Bern, North Carolina.

Unfortunately, upon reaching America, the Gillespie lads, like other humble freedom-loving Presbyterians discovered, as in England, the Crown's aristocratic Anglicans had imposed their Kingly Rights on America's colonists. Having fought for their religious rights for many centuries, the Gillespie family, like all Presbyterians, were especially disturbed that England's monarchy continued to control their individual liberties.

The Crown forced the English Anglican Church's imposed, corrupt, tithes down their throats. Most often the tithes were appropriated by the local church officials.

When the young Gillespie lads reached the Carolina shores, they received much care from many Presbyterian family friends whose ancestors fought alongside the Gillespies in Scotland's Covenanter crusade for freedom and in Ulster's horrific Londonderry siege.

Earlier in 1736, a large number of Scots-Irish Presbyterians, sponsored by a rich London merchant Henry McCulloch, emigrated from Ulster to the Duplin County North Carolina countryside to settle on McCulloch land grants from King George II. These Duplin Presbyterians were among the earliest to settle in North Carolina. They named their settlement and Presbyterian meetinghouse, the Grove. The 1736 Grove Presbyterian Church was the first Presbyterian Church in North Carolina.

Shortly after the Scots-Irish from Ulster settled their Village of Grove, they built their Grove Presbyterian meetinghouse. A few years after the Ulster Scots Irish settled the Village of Grove, Minister McAden moved to North Carolina to minister the Presbyterians around the Eastern North Carolina countryside.

Similar to the many other Presbyterian Scots-Irish communities throughout the colonies, the Village of Grove built their log Church that became the Village's vital center for religious, social, and political activity. Soon the church was fortunate, the Presbyterian synod of Philadelphia assigned the vibrant Minister McAden as their pastor. As customary, the Church served as a center for political activity meetings for the community to discuss their many opinions and ideas for supporting the founding of a new nation. From the pulpit, McAden, like all of the brave colonial Presbyterian ministers, warned of the evils of "Kingly Rights" and so vividly reminded their parishioners of their Covenanter forefather's suffering. Their Church provided a sanctuary for the members to discuss freely their moral right to rebel against the unjust policies of government.

The Grove worshipers were pleased that they had a place to worship to escape the discrimination of the Anglican English aristocrats.

McAden was born in Pennsylvania of parents from Monaghan County, Ulster Ireland. McAden was a graduate of the Presbyterian Seminary College of New Jersey, today's Princeton University. McAden married a Miss Scott from Virginia and they had seven children. Like the McAdens, Gillespies and Pearsalls most of Carolina's Scots-Irish emigrated from Ulster.

In 1759, Duplin's Grove Presbyterian Church selected McAden as their pastor. For ten years, McAden faithfully served the Grove congregation.

Over the years in Ulster, McAden's ancestors were close friends of the David Gillespie family. Hugh McAden his wife, and other former Ulster Presbyterian family friends from Ulster, Ireland ensured much care and support for the Gillespie lads' early years in colonial America. Soon Borthick, longing for his home in Ulster, returned to Ireland. James, as a teenager worked as an apprentice for a Richland's Onslow County tanner.

In the early 1760's, Reverend McAden encouraged and supported James Gillespie's move to the Presbyterian Grove settlement of Duplin County. In 1763 young James purchased land with a small home from Thomas Routledge. He now owned his first property in America, located one mile east of the Scots-Irish Grove settlement.

James named his first home in America "Golden Grove". In 1764, McAden sold to his family friend, young James Gillespie, 465 acres to add to his plantation. James remodeled his house into a two-story colonial home. In the early 1770's, prior to the Revolutionary War, James received a number of land patents totaling several thousand acres along the North East Cape Fear River from colonial Governor Josiah Martin that greatly enlarged his plantation, Golden Grove.

A few years following the sale of his 465-acre homestead to James Gillespie, McAden left the Duplin area to preach in Caswell County, North Carolina. He preached at the Red House Presbyterian meetinghouse until his death in 1781. McAden died two weeks before Cornwallis troops ransacked and looted his home. The British destroyed nearly all of McAden's ministry records except for his diary.

His diary told of his preaching tour from Cross Creek down the Cape Fear River to Bladen County. His diary describes the warm welcome he received from the Thomas Roberson family at their Walnut Grove home, a few miles west of Elizabethtown, along the south bank of the Cape Fear River.

Following his teenage years, Archibald Gillespie settled in the town of Bogue, which today is Swansboro. In 1772, Archibald bought a ½-acre lot in Bogue from Theophilus Weeks, the founder of the town of Swansboro. He opened a tavern and served spirits to Bogue's local seafarers. In 1773 Bogue Inlet appointed Archibald as inspector for their maritime operations. Archibald married a lady from Swansboro with whom he had three children: Borthick, Clement and Catherine.

James Gillespie's older brother, David III, never came to America. He wrote James a number of letters from Shantine that are preserved in the Wright-Gillespie Papers of the University of North Carolina's Southern Historical Collection.

James' sister, Jane, married a Mr. McMurray. They lived in Shantine and raised a daughter Catherine who married a Mr. Coultery. Catherine had no children and upon death, she willed her Scottish property to James Gillespie's two sons, David and Joseph.

James returned to Ireland in the early 1760's and received a classical education from the University of Dublin.

After building his Golden Grove Plantation, on October 11, 1770, James Gillespie married Dorcus Mumford of Richlands, North Carolina. James met Dorcus soon after he arrived in America and the two grew up in Richlands. Dorcus was the daughter of Joseph Mumford Jr. and Mildred Wright. James and Dorcus' marriage bond was a marriage contract, apparently to protect the Mumford land holdings upon the early death of Dorcus.

James and Dorcus raised seven children: Catherine born December 26, 1771, David born April 5, 1774, Lucy born March 14, 1776, Joseph born February 19, 1779, Elizabeth born February 28, 1781, Jane born March 19, 1785, and Mildred born Sep 17, 1789. Joseph and Catherine were Mumford orphans James and Dorcus adopted early in their marriage.

Chapter 12
The Presbyterian Rebellion (The Revolutionary War)

The British Parliament during the early 1770's sought compensation for the Seven Years War (1756-1763) in which the British drove the French effectively from most of North America. For repayment, King George began forcing many unfair taxes on the Colonies.

When George enacted his famous Stamp Act, the colonies decided to take whatever measures necessary to limit future unjust acts by the Crown. The Stamp Act collected direct tax revenues on all paper products and documents such as deeds, court documents, and marriage licenses. Each paper product contained a stamped label that indicated the tax the Colonist owed to the Crown. The Patriots in revenge, disguised as Indians, held their famous tea party and dumped King George's tea into the Boston harbor. King George was enraged.

Following the famous Boston Tea Party, and the battle of Lexington and Concord, in April 1775, the war began. The colonies without any army or navy declared their independence and war against a very powerful, populous and wealthy nation. The colonies no longer needed England's power for defense from France or the Indians.

England crushed King Louis of France and with a harsh hand had crushed Prince Charlie and the Jacobites hopes at Culloden. Her mighty fleets controlled the seas. The population of the thirteen colonies was approximate two million. One third of the colony's citizens supported the Crown. Many Colonial Americans were Tories, especially the large plantation owners of the South. These Tories had received large land grants, over the years from the English Kings, and were faithful to the Crown. The plantation owners were totally dependent on the English for a market for their farm products, and they especially needed English mills to refine their cotton.

The Patriots realized if their rebellion against the Crown failed they faced hanging for treason. Many colonists were descendants of Scots-Irish Covenanters. Ancestors of these freedom loving emigrants had suffered terribly over the centuries from the cruelties of England's Kings. Having suffered so long from the cruelties of the English Crown, these ever determined Patriots fully understood their revolutionary fight was worth the effort. They firmly believed and knew there was no other choice but to fight. Like Patrick Henry's famous saying, the brave Scots-Irish believed, "Give me Liberty or Give me Death".

They were willing to hang together or hang separately in their fight for freedom. Unlike some colonists of the day they didn't need to be convinced by Thomas Payne's "Common Sense" essay that England's Royal Ruffians were rotten to the core. For many years their ancestors had experienced, first hand, cruelties inflicted under the Crown's Kingly Rule.

Early in the Revolution, Thomas Payne brought from England to America his Common Sense philosophy. His "Common Sense" widely distributed essays vigorously preached against the English Crown's "Kingly Rule". Payne, in his Common Sense publication stated, "All Kings are blasphemous usurpers who boldly claim their sovereign authority over all other human beings that rightly only belong to God".

The mighty Presbyterian theologians, including Patrick Gillespie and Samuel Rutherford followed by John Locke, had fervently preached their resounding Covenanter philosophy, "The King should serve the people and that Law is King (Lex Rex)." In America, the Scots-Irish Presbyterians did not have to be persuaded to fight the Redcoats in a war against British General Cornwallis. Many English Parliament members, referred to the

Revolutionary War as the "Presbyterian Rebellion". Fight they did; especially, Carolina's Scots-Irish back woodsmen formerly from Ulster.

Following the Battles of Lexington and Concord, George Washington arrived in Boston, in July 1775, to take command of the Continental Army. The Patriots positioned heavy cannons on Dorchester heights that overlooked the British Army and convinced General Howe to flee to Nova Scotia.

Using Canada as a safe haven, Howe reorganized his forces and returned with refreshed troops to Long Island where he prepared his Army for an invasion of Washington's forces camped on Manhattan. In the largest battle of the Revolution, Howe drove Washington from Manhattan to Brooklyn Heights. Howe captured Brooklyn Heights and drove Washington to White Plains. On the run, Washington marched his Army into New Jersey leaving Howe in control of New York City, including White Plains, and Manhattan Island's Fort Washington, (near today's George Washington Bridge).

Howe, in his New York campaign, captured several thousand colonial troops. The British imprisoned them on their offshore sailing war ships. Howe's prison ships were the beginning of the British prison ship system. In the following four years more Patriot prisoners died of disease and malnutrition than in all the battles of the war.

Cornwallis chased Washington through New Jersey, across the Delaware River, into Pennsylvania. Both armies withdrew and settled in for the long cold winter of 1776.

When Howe captured Philadelphia, the Colonial Congress escaped and moved their meeting headquarters to York, Pennsylvania.

Washington, with his Patriot troops, spent a starving winter at Valley Forge with a shortage of food, clothes, and military supplies. Martha Custis Washington and other heroic colonial women like Kitty Greene, wife of Nathaniel

Greene, led a patriotic campaign to provide critical food and clothing for the frozen and starved Valley Forge troops. These brave colonial women endured the freezing weather to visit the encamped Patriots in a desperate effort to improve troop morale. Morale was especially low considering Washington had blindfolded and shot a number of deserters before a firing squad to discourage further desertions. Obviously, there was a critical need for improved troop morale. During this terrible Valley Forge winter, over 2500 of Washington's troops died from starvation and freezing.

When the colonial government left Philadelphia for York, Pennsylvania, General Howe spent the cold, snowy, winter of 1776 in Philadelphia. Over the winter, he enjoyed the sexual favors of a Mrs. Loring.

Fortunately, for General Washington and the freezing Patriots, Howe chose to enjoy the pleasures of Mrs. Loring over the winter rather than attack the starving defenseless Patriot army. Her favors, provided to Howe, obviously ensured her husband gained a higher rank in the British army. Many Colonials view Mrs. Loring's whoring, providing pleasures to Howe throughout the winter, as exceedingly Patriotic and heroic. Her many pleasures detained Howe over the winter, thus he was too busily preoccupied to attack the freezing, starving and defenseless Patriots at Valley Forge.

British General Howe in his New York campaign captured over 5000 Patriots. With huge losses of troops from desertion, capture and casualties the Continental Army was in dire need of troops. The Patriot military situation appeared hopeless with fewer than 5,000 troops remaining.

Fortunately for America, British General Burgoyne suffered a major loss at the Battle of Saratoga. The Battle of Saratoga commanded by General Gates and Benedict Arnold was the turning battle of the war. Arnold's command was instrumental in America's Saratoga victory. To the amazement and disbelief of Arnold, Gates, with his huge political support, received most of the credit for the Saratoga victory.

Following the encouraging colonial victory at Saratoga, the French entered the war in full support of the revolutionaries. Lord Clinton, in command of Howe's troops, decided to move the British Army South to gain support of the large plantation owners.

Chapter 13
General, Lord, Clinton Moves the British Army to the South

Many of the southern plantation owners were Loyalists and the British counted on many of these Loyalists to support King George III. In February 1776, General Clinton invaded the American South with two thousand men supported by a naval squadron. Fortunately, for North Carolina, the Tories decisive victory at Moore's Creek, early in the war, crushed the Loyalist support in and around the Wilmington countryside. The Whigs key victory at Moore's Creek kept the British out of their countryside for several years. Their victory moved the British invasion further south.

A number of Jacobites fled to America, following the Battle of Culloden, and settled in the Cross Creek area of North Carolina. Predominantly Catholic, these Jacobites continuously supported a Stuart retake of the English throne. These Jacobites sympathized with the Scots-Irish Highlanders and were not welcome by the Scots- Irish Presbyterians. Flora McDonald, the Scottish maiden from Scotland's Isle of Skye, had assisted Bonnie Prince Charlie, and the Jacobites. To enhance their opportunities in America, these Highlanders shrewdly sided with the Colonial Loyalists. Flora signed an oath of alliance with the Loyalist cause and obtained land from King George III.

Flora and her husband, Allan, helped with organizing the Tory troops in and around Cross Creek. The Whigs captured Allan, Flora's husband, at Moore's Creek and threw Allan from one jail to the next. He eventually ended up in a New York prison. Allan was unsure of his fate, while Flora was unaware of his condition or whereabouts. Like other captured Loyalists, the McDonalds' lives were ruined. The Whigs also captured Flora's son, Alexander, during the battle of Moore's Creek and imprisoned him with his father Allan. The Whigs determined to get even, constantly harassed the McDonalds, and confiscated their property that King George III granted to them for their loyalty. In 1781 shortly after Flora reunited with her son and husband Allan, in New York, they gladly returned to Scotland's highlands.

The British loss at Moore's Creek encouraged the British to move south to Charles Town where Clinton's initial attack was unsuccessful. Following his failure to take Charles Town in 1778, Clinton cleverly sailed his Army south and captured Savannah. Clinton next sailed back north, captured and occupied Charles Town (now Charleston), the South's largest city and seaport.

During this period, King George III promoted Cornwallis as commander of the British Southern Army. Shortly after Gates arrived in Charles Town, the Continental Congress appointed Gates commander of the Southern Patriot Army. Gates selection was against the wishes of George Washington who shared his concerns with the Continental Congress to no avail.

Cornwallis and Gates prepared their respective troops for the battle of Camden. Gates made the strategic mistake of engaging the British in direct frontal line formation without bayonets. The Battle of Camden was a disaster for the Patriots. Gates fled from the battlefield, after the first charge by the British, in a cowardly retreat. Washington made his famous remark, "We Americans recognize Gates as the General that rode further and faster away from the dangers of battle than any other Patriot soldier in the war." Cornwallis captured many Patriot troops and imprisoned them on the dreaded British prison ships off the Carolina coastline.

Cornwallis chased the colonial army across the South Carolina countryside to the Battle of Waxhaws where his beastly Cavalry commander, Bannister Tarleton, defeated the Patriots. At Waxhaw, Tarleton murdered many

Patriots who had surrendered with their weapons down and hands up in the air. His savage killing of these brave Scots-Irishmen increased the fire in the fighting spirit of the remaining revolutionaries. Soon, these brave Patriots used their anger as a blazing torch to create a raging fire-storm that would soon drive Cornwallis' Redcoats out of the Carolinas.

Cornwallis continued chasing the Patriots around in circles across the Carolina's. Meanwhile, the Scots-Irish, rugged mountaineers, heroically defeated British Major Patrick Ferguson at Kings Mountain, S. C. In the Kings Mountain battle, there were six Gillespies, including two Captains and one Colonel. Several of these King's Mountain Gillespies were close relatives of John Gillespie from Clifton Forge, Virginia who supplied the born-fighting Scots-Irish mountain men with his father William's famed Gillespie rifle. John's father, William Gillespie, earlier in Virginia, had begun making his accurate long barreled firearms in the 1740's. Conveniently, William's brother Robert operated a powder works nearby and assisted with the making of Gillespie rifles.

Following Kings Mountain, the Scots-Irish, under General Morgan, decisively defeated Tarleton at the Battle of Cowpens. At Cowpens, Daniel Morgan exhibited the finest military tactics of the war. Unfortunately, Morgan severely injured his back in battle and retired from the colonial army.

Washington was frustrated over Gates' disastrous and cowardly performance at the battle of Camden. Without hesitation, Washington handpicked Nathaniel Greene to command his Colonial Southern troops. Nathaniel Greene, from Rhode Island, and his flirtatious wife, Kitty, were close friends and socialites of George and Martha Washington.

Greene led Cornwallis in circles across the

Carolina's many swamps. He outran the Redcoats and refused to engage his enemy without sufficient food and munitions. Finally, Greene maneuvered his Army across the Dan River into Virginia. In Virginia Greene found a huge welcoming party. These South-West Virginia Scots-Irish mountain families, including the Gillespies with their superior long rifles, happily provided these brave colonial patriots with much-needed supplies. With food and armaments, Greene brought his army roaring back into Mecklenburg County, North Carolina. Greene chose his moment and battleground at Guilford Courthouse to face Cornwallis. Greene found Cornwallis encamped on Presbyterian Minister Caldwell's estate.

Shortly after setting up camp on Minister Caldwell's farm, Cornwallis ordered his troops to burn the reverend's extensive library and all ministry records. The British accused the Presbyterian Church and ministers of holding community meetings to organize attacks against the many British camps around the Guilford countryside.

Greene commanded the battle at Guilford Courthouse with Mecklenburg's freedom loving, Scots-Irish, troops. Among these determined troops were the Gillespie brothers, Colonel Daniel, and Captain John Gillespie. Green's tactics copied those so successfully deployed by Morgan at Cowpens, with militia in the frontal assault backed by Continentals and his cavalry in reserve.

Cornwallis launched a ferocious frontal attack. The Patriot's militia at first fell back. Suddenly the Patriots charged forward, which frustrated Cornwallis, and he in turn ordered his artillery to charge forward into the Patriot troops. The battle became a confusing hand-to-hand combat. Cornwallis desperately tried to turn the tide of battle. Exasperated, Cornwallis ordered his cannons to fire grape shot directly into the entangled hand-to-hand melee wherein he killed both Patriots and British alike. England's King Edward I, over four centuries earlier, used a similar strategy against William Wallace when he ordered his Welsh archers to rain arrows down on the battle.

Green withdrew his troops from the battlefield and left Cornwallis and his many dead and wounded with an empty victory.

After the strong resistance of the Scots-Irish backwoodsmen and a near defeat, Cornwallis was convinced that his ragged, poorly supplied, Army needed a rest from the savage fighting of the Scots-Irish. Cornwallis with his bedraggled soldiers marched through Hillsboro on his way to Wilmington. They marched down the east bank of the Cape Fear River, down the old Wilmington road past Cross Creek, and Elizabethtown. The British stopped briefly at the old Carvers Creek, Quaker meeting house to rest under the shade of the large oak trees. They replenished their canteens with creek water and stole corn meal from the old Carvers Creek grist mill operated by the Quakers.

Cornwallis freed many slaves and stole several hundred horses as he marched through the Cape Fear River valley. Cornwallis's troops in rags, and wearing rough hand sewn cowhide shoes, finally reached the safe haven in Wilmington secured by Major Craig.

With Cornwallis in Wilmington, the invasion of the New Hanover and Duplin County North Carolina countryside began.

Chapter 14
Revolutionary Battles of Duplin's Heroic Patriots

Under the War Act of November 25, 1776, Col. William Dickson, Col Routledge and Col James Kenan, assisted by many Duplin Patriotic citizens, organized the local Patriot militia. Duplin's militia earlier participated in the victory at Moore's Creek. Other leading Duplin militia organizers included the Dicksons, Gillespies, Stallings, Routledges, Pearsalls, Bourneys, Hudsons and Moores. Under the War Act of November 25, 1776, the first battalion of North Carolina Volunteers commissioned James Gillespie as a Captain and authorized his command of a volunteer light horse cavalry. His cavalry's main mission was to prevent Tory encampments in and around Duplin County. Early in the war the British did not occupy Wilmington, thus, there was only a limited British presence and few skirmishes in Eastern North Carolina. Early in the war, the main danger were the menacing Tory encampments throughout the countryside.

Mixed with James Gillespie's busy legislative duties as a delegate to the Halifax Capital, and later his administrative support to acting Governor Martin, James Gillespie was especially busy throughout the war. His cavalry duties included routing Tories from various local encampments in Duplin County including Sacreta, Goshen-Woodwards Chase, Six Runs, Cohera and Turkey. To reward James for several years of heroically leading his cavalry against the local Tories, the Continental Army commissioned James Gillespie a Major. In 1779, with Cornwallis' arrival in Charles Town, Gillespie for a brief period assisted with the futile defense of the City against General Clinton's British troops.

In 1781 when the British captured Wilmington, the

Loyalists and British became especially dangerous in the Duplin County countryside. The British officer Major James Craig commanded the British in their countryside attacks around Duplin County and the town of Wilmington.

A well-known military mission in August of 1781 that Major James Gillespie and his loyal Duplin militia helped organize was the "Tory Hole" battle. Colonel Thomas Roberson of Bladen called upon his friend and comrade Major James Gillespie and Duplin volunteers under his command to rout the Tories out of their encampment in Elizabethtown where they continuously staged attacks on the local Bladen Patriots. Colonel Roberson, his brother Capt. Peter Roberson, and Major Gillespie along with sixty-eight ragged, but determined, soldiers waded across the Cape Fear River in pre-dawn hours. They knew there were four hundred Tories and fortunately they knew much more detail about the Tory encampment through a Whig spy, Sally Salter. Mrs. Salter had posed a day earlier as a woman selling eggs. Mrs. Salter informed the Whig militia led by Colonel Roberson and Major Gillespie of the number of Whig prisoners and reported several prisoners possessed hidden weapons. Mrs. Salter also spotted the dreaded loyalist Colonel Fanning in the encampment on his way with prisoners to Wilmington.

Earlier, Fanning over the winter burned Peter Roberson's home as well as that of Thomas Roberson's Walnut Grove family plantation. Fanning burned Peter Roberson's home and cruelly forced his wife and young infant child into the freezing snow. A few days later Peter's young baby boy and wife died. Learning of Fanning's location, the Whigs, especially the Roberson brothers, were anxious to kill Fanning for his many murderous deeds.

During the night of August 27, 1781 under the command of Colonel Thomas Roberson, Bladen's patriotic Whigs prepared to attack Colonel Slingsby's camp. The Tories held captive a number of Patriot prisoners from their earlier raid on the Cumberland County Courthouse. The Patriots prepared to cross the Cape Fear River, which fortunately was only neck deep due to an ongoing drought. They crossed the river holding their rifles and clothes over their heads. These ragged Patriots redressed and prepared their muskets for the battle that was soon to begin.

As the moon set, in total darkness, Gillespie and the Roberson brothers led the ferocious Whig attack, shouting "Washington". With total surprise, they fired from all directions upon the Tory encampment. Joyfully the Whig prisoners joined in the onslaught. The Patriots attacked and within seconds killed the Tory officers. The encampment, believing Washington's entire Army was attacking, with uncontrollable fear jumped off a steep cliff into a deep ravine. The victorious Whigs in fear of a major retaliatory Tory attack grabbed all of their captured guns and supplies and hastily led their freed prisoners back across the Cape Fear River to safety.

Bladen Patriots remembered the ferociously fought Elizabethtown battle, led by Gillespie and the Roberson brothers as the "Tory Hole" battle. Their decisive victory, for a brief period, deterred the attacks of the Tories on the Bladen County and the Cape Fear region. Fortunately for Fanning, he had left the Tory encampment the night before to take several Patriot prisoners to Wilmington.

In September 1781, shortly after the Roberson and Gillespie victorious Tory battle, Colonel Fanning and Hector McNeil led one of their more successful Carolina Tory raids on Hillsboro, the North Carolina Capital. Fanning and McNeil captured Patriot Governor Burke. Following their victorious raid, Major James Craig marched out to Livingston Creek, several miles west of Wilmington, to meet Fanning, and to pick up their prized prisoner.

Upon hearing of Burke's capture, General Butler, late that evening, sent Major Gillespie's light horse cavalry out in an attempt to rescue the Governor. The Patriot cavalry ran into the British Calvary several miles up the Duplin road. Due to darkness, both sides disengaged. Craig escorted his prisoner Burke to Wilmington and imprisoned him in a downtown home without any bedding or furniture. Shortly thereafter, Major Craig moved Governor Burke to Charles Town where the British paroled him on James Island.

Captain Peter Roberson, a hero during the Elizabethtown "Tory Hole" battle, was called bloody Peter by the Tories because he kept no prisoners. He killed all Tories and British he captured. On one such occasion, Captain "Bloody" Peter Roberson and his Bladen County Militia were about to execute two Tories. One of the Tories kept asking for more time to pray. Fortunately as he was praying, God answered his prayer. Up rode Hector McNeil, a leading Tory, and attacked Roberson. The prisoner escaped during McNeil's skirmish with Roberson.

Throughout the American Revolution, the Grove Village Scots- Irish clan including the Gillespies, Stallings, Dicksons, Pearsalls and Routledges were especially close knit. The Grove Clan (clachnan) hated the Tories and the British. They remembered centuries of terrible persecution inflicted on their ancestors by the English Crown. Colonels James Kenan, Thomas Routledge and William Dickson, with their militia, continually attacked the hated Tory Loyalists and British soldiers. The Carolinas suffered a vindictive civil war where old scores were settled with more bloodshed and destruction.

Colonel Thomas Routledge at the outbreak of the war served as a member of the Wilmington Safety Committee. The North Carolina War Act authorized Duplin's Militia and commissioned a number of their local gentry as officers. At this time, the War Act commissioned Thomas Routledge as a Major, who soon was promoted to Colonel. During the battle to defend Charles Town from

General Clinton's southern invasion, the British captured Colonel Routledge. Routledge's escape from his Charles Town captivity was very fortunate since the British soon imprisoned all their captives aboard British prison ships in the Charles Town bay. The treatment aboard the ships' prisons was horrific. Many of the American captives soon died from disease. Many wives, sisters and daughters made the long trip to Charles Town with food and medicine to aid their loved ones. Their kind efforts saved many prisoners from dying. After escaping, Routledge returned to Duplin to fight the British in the surrounding countryside with his dragoons. With real swords unavailable, they handmade such weapons from cross cut saws. Included among their handmade arms were hickory and oak staffs, and spears. His mounted dragoons, numbering seventy Whigs, earned their name the "Knock 'em Down Men" as they effectively fought the Tories around the countryside.

One of James Gillespie's early acquaintances in the war, and with whom he later served in Congress, was Colonel Timothy Bloodworth. Colonials in and around Wilmington knew Senator Bloodworth as a "jack of all trades" and an outstanding gunsmith.

In July of 1781, Bloodworth was hunting on Negro Head Point, across the Cape Fear River from the main downtown wharf of Wilmington, when he lost his favorite coon dog, "Old Blue". Searching for "Old Blue", Bloodworth accidentally fell into a huge and hollow cypress tree stump adjacent to the riverbank. He did not find "Old Blue", but instead, he was amazed at the size of the old cypress stump and the excellent concealment that the tree hollow provided.

Bloodworth, like all Carolina Patriots, was much concerned over the Redcoats menacing occupation and enjoyment of the fineries of downtown Wilmington. He soon recognized his newly discovered cypress bunker provided an excellent and well concealed location to harass the British across the river as they entered the wharf's taverns. Using his excellent gunsmith skills, Bloodworth machined a special long barreled rifle capable of sniping across the Cape Fear River. Several days later before dawn, Bloodworth and his young son quietly rowed down the river from their Burgaw plantation to his secret cypress hideaway. In the morning hours as British soldiers began entering shops along the wharf, Bloodworth's sniping began. He and his son enjoyed taking turns shooting at the British for most of the day. At nightfall, Bloodworth and his teenage son left their hideaway and cautiously rowed back up the North East Cape Fear River to their Burgaw Plantation. The Red Coats never discovered from where the many shots were fired or that the Bloodworths were responsible for wounding their British adversaries with their specially adapted long rifle he named "Old Betsy". "Old Betsy", remained with Bloodworth's descendants for many years.

In early 1781 with General Cornwallis headquartered in Wilmington, many Tory and British soldiers were encamped in and around the nearby Duplin countryside. Their presence created an increasingly dangerous threat.

During this time, as recorded by Colonel William Dickson in his letters preserved in the Library of Congress, the British overran the Duplin countryside. They looted and burned as they marched.

The Tories and their women followed the British destruction and stole anything they could cart away. The women rode sidesaddle and like later Civil War carpetbaggers took jewelry, linens, silverware and anything else of value. After the war, William Dickson wrote a diary which described how the Duplin countryside was looted and burned by the British and Tory allies. Dickson explained how the Redcoats ransacked and burned the Village Grove homes of James Gillespie and William

Houston.

Due to his constant attacks on the local Tory encampments and his Tory Hole battle that killed many Tories, Major Gillespie was a number one enemy of British Major Craig. In retaliation, during the first week of August 1781 shortly after James' victorious attack, Major Craig came to Duplin for a few days. William Dickson in his Library of Congress letters describes Major Craig's looting and burning. Craig looted and burned James Gillespie's Golden Grove Plantation to ashes along with that of Lt. Houston's home. During his three-day encampment in Duplin, Craig occupied Colonel Routledge's home, which was adjacent to today's Routledge Cemetery. Surprisingly, Major Craig left Colonel Routledge's home intact.

Gillespie's wife, Dorcus, managed to escape into the snake infested, muddy and briar entangled Maxwell swamp with their five small children. These included five-month-old Elizabeth, ten-year-old Catherine, seven-year-old David, five-year-old Lucy, and two-year-old Joseph. Cathy, David, and Lucy with their mother carried baby Elizabeth and the two-year-old toddler, Joseph, into the woods. They outran the advancing British as the Redcoats crashed in the front door of their plantation.

After Major Craig and his scoundrels departed the Grove countryside to plunder New Bern, Dorcus Gillespie quietly came out of hiding from the swamp with her five young children. She knocked at the backdoor of her close friends, the William Dicksons. James returned from brief N. C. legislative duties with the House of Commons finding his family safe with the Dicksons. His home was burned to cinders.

Following Fannon's capture of Governor Burke in September of 1781, Gillespie for several months provided administrative assistance to acting Governor Martin who was constantly moving around with his large trunk of state government records to avoid capture. During his service with Governor Martin, James Gillespie boarded his family with the William Dickson family. Following the war with the help of their many Scots- Irish friends, the Gillespies built their new home along Marsh Creek.

Chapter 15
The Heroic Role of the Scots-Irish in America's Fight for FREEDOM

Like the closely knitted clan of Scots- Irish from Duplin's Grove that included the Gillespies, Dicksons, Pearsalls and Routledges, the Scots-Irish across colonial America played a significant role in America's quest for "FREEDOM".

George Washington greatly admired his Scots -Irish troops and stated, "I will take my stand with the Scots-Irish in Virginia and Carolina." They provided one-half of the Revolutionary war troops and earned the appointment of twenty-five of George Washington's Generals.

America's Declaration of Independence was printed by John Dunlop, first signed by John Hancock, and read aloud by Colonel Nixon to his fellow patriots. All of these Presbyterian Scots- Irish were courageous freedom fighters who risked their lives and their property for independence from the English Crown. The Scots-Irish Virginia legislator Patrick Henry proclaimed, "I know not what course others may take, but give me liberty or give me death."

Prior to America's Declaration of Independence on July 4, 1776, the Scots-Irish of Lancaster Pennsylvania in June 1774 wrote their Hanover Resolve which denounced British tyranny. A year later in May 1775, the Ulster Scots-Irish of Mecklenburg County, under the leadership of Abraham Alexander, wrote their Declaration of Independence in the halls of their small Charlottetown, Liberty Hall School. The Mecklenburg Declaration was the first Declaration of Independence signed for freedom from England.

A key beginning for America's Liberty and Independence was the Scots-Irish, largely Presbyterian, battle of Alamance against British appointed Governor Tryon's oppressive and crooked county and state legislators in North Carolina.

Marjoleine Kars's book, "Breaking Loose Together", provides an excellent summary of the economics, religion, and politics surrounding the Regulator battle. (The backwoods Scots-Irish were referred to as "Regulators" as they desperately tried to convince Governor Tryon to regulate fairly the laws of North Carolina) Kar's book describes the horrific treatment of the poor down-trodden mostly Scots- Irish farmers by government officials led by Tryon. Reverend David Caldwell with much diplomacy tried hard, but to no avail, to convince Tryon and his crooked officials to treat the Scots-Irish farmers fairly.

The Regulator's battle for Liberty and Freedom provided a catalyst for the other colonies striking a spark that spread like a wild forest fire with determination across the countryside which eventually drove British General Cornwallis out of the North Carolina Piedmont. The Scots-Irish Battle of the Regulators prompted these staunch supporters of freedom, a few years later, to sign their Mecklenburg Declaration.

The Regulator conflict involved a futile effort by mostly Presbyterian Scots-Irish farmers to prevent crooked government officials from swindling their homesteads. These Scots- Irish had struggled long and hard for their land and homes in America.

Henry McCulloch, a Scottish merchant in 1737 convinced an English Privy Council under King George II to grant him and several silent partners an 1875 square mile land grant. His speculating scheme was to obtain a selfish fortune that involved charging unending quit-rents to the Scots-Irish immigrants pouring into the Carolina backwoods.

His son, Henry Eustace McCulloch arrived in 1764 in Mecklenburg County with a band of his roguish friends to survey their granted land and to begin charging large quit-rents. Henry junior's lust for money and young Scots-

Irish lasses was huge. McCulloch's pursuit for both was to impose major problems on these freedom loving farmers who for the most part had recently emigrated to America to escape the Crown's corruptions. When the poor farmers were unable to pay his demanded quit-rents, McCulloch slaughtered their cows and hogs for sale on the pork and beef markets. If the down-trodden farmer had no collateral to forfeit, McCulloch many times forgave the month's rent for sexual favors. He usually demanded his choice of the farmer's daughters.

Reverend Alexander Craighead, preaching at Sugar Creek and Rocky River, desperately tried to convince colonial Governor Tryon that Scotland's "Solemn League and Covenant", signed by the Stuart Kings, denied King George the authority to impose the poor desperate Scots-Irish farmers quit-rent. He explained that both King Charles I and II faithfully signed and accepted Scotland's Covenant in the 17th century. "The Divine Rights of Kings', so bitterly opposed by Gillespie, Rutherford and the many other Covenanters, in the 17th century, continued to plague the freedom loving Scots-Irish in America. (If only the Covenanters had followed the Gillespie's advice and not supported Charles II, allowing his escape to France, Cromwell could have also beheaded Charles II for treason. With the death of Charles II there wouldn't have been any corrupting Carolina land grant bribes. With no Lord Proprietors in America, the Scots-Irish farmers would not have been swindled out of their justly deserved homesteads.)

The swindlers soon discovered how difficult it was to control the liberties of these born- fighting Scots-Irishmen. Having abandoned their homes in Ulster for liberties promised in America, the Scots-Irish were determined to protect their homes in America.

William Husband, a key leader against the Regulators, drew up a list of complaints of the farmers fight for justice against Governor Tryon's fraudulent actions. He desperately tried to get Tryon to recognize their complaints, but Tryon ignored them all. Other participants in the Alamance Regulator battle were the Gillespie brothers, Daniel and John Gillespie, descendants of the Gillespie family that led Scotland's renowned Covenanters in their Solemn League and Covenant Crusade.

Governor Tryon's crooked colonial officials intentionally lost tax records and collected more and continually higher taxes. In May 1771, Tryon's roguish militia severely beat and murdered several of the poor, oppressed and unarmed Scots-Irish farmers. Tryon imprisoned six of these poor and humble farmers in Hillsboro. Several days later, in a mock hanging just east of town overlooking the Eno River, Tryon hanged his helpless captives. A number of the other Regulators were severely beaten, and others imprisoned. Other Regulators, fortunate enough to evade capture, escaped to the Cumberland Valley in today's Tennessee.

Governor Tryon made his own selfish use of the large sums he swindled from the poor downtrodden Scots-Irish. He used his stolen funds to build a luxurious mansion on the banks of New Bern's Neuse River that is still today known and visited by tourists as Tryon's Palace.

- TRYON'S PALACE -
British Governor Tryon's Palace built with funds stolen

from the Scots-Irish farmers

The Regulators requested thirteen reforms from Governor Tryon. When North Carolina's delegates drafted North Carolina's Constitution at Halifax, the Presbyterian Scots-Irish delegates insisted that all of their Alamance reforms to protect the rights of the common man be included.

The Battle of Kings Mountain was a significant turning point in the Revolution. In the Colonial Patriots savage fight at Kings Mountain these born fighting Scots-Irish defeated twice their size British force and captured over a one thousand loyalists. All five colonels in this Colonial victory were Presbyterian Scots- Irish.

At Kings Mountain, the Gillespies fought savagely, leading their fellow backcountry Scots-Irishmen in a relentless attack against opposition leader Ferguson.

Colonel George Gillespie heroically supported the battle with his relative William Gillespies' famous Gillespie long mountain rifle.

The Gillespie Rifle

Colonel Gillespie, prior to battle, likely obtained critically needed gun powder from the Gillespie's Clifton Forge powder works. He led his regiment that fought valiantly that included four Gillespie relatives: Jacob Gillespie, James Gillespie, Captain Thomas Gillespie and Captain William Gillespie.

Chapter 16
King George Declared, "This War is a Presbyterian Rebellion"

King George and the English Parliament looked upon the American Revolutionary War as the Presbyterian's War and a huge Scots-Irish Presbyterian rebellion. The British considered the Presbyterian Church as the house of evil acting against the Crown. Over the course of the war from 1775 to 1781, the British troops burned over seventy Presbyterian churches. Such an atrocity was portrayed in the Mel Gibson movie, "The Patriot". The movie portrayed Tarleton's cavalry locking the doors of the Waxhaw Presbyterian Church with its full congregation, including women and children, inside before the building was put to torch. The Presbyterian's used their Churches to hold community gatherings to decide how to deal with the Tory and British attacks and their encampments in their countryside.

Irishmen say that over one third of the Protestants in Ireland came to America in the 1700's. Many sought safety from the Ulster famine, Queen Anne's Test Act, and the cruel repressions of their landlords. The British Crown ruthlessly crushed the protestant revolts over the Crown's Test Acts in Ulster that forced the Anglican Church on the citizens. Many Protestant leaders were hanged. Over ¼ to ½ million Scots- Irish migrated in fewer than fifty years. In the mid 1700's in the South Carolina backcountry, the Scots-Irish began arriving by droves into the counties of York, Breckenridge, Lancaster, and Chester. They settled in communal and clannish family groups similar to their Irish homeland communities (Clachans).

The Great Religious Awakening of the 1740's led by Jonathan Edwards, George Whitefield, and Gilbert Tennant with their log churches across New England, set afire the Presbyterian's zeal for religious freedom and liberties. The thundering sermons of these mighty Scots-

Irish theologians enforced the fighting spirit of colonial patriots. These freedom-seeking Scots-Irish viewed the Revolution as America's Holy War. Whitefield and Tennant's philosophical preaching influenced the political and religious philosophies of the majority of America's founders, especially Benjamin Rush who led the Continental Congress.

The aristocrats established the Anglican Church as the Crown's official religion for the colonies. King George sent Charles Woodmason, an Anglican minister, into the South Carolina backcountry in an attempt to influence the Scots-Irish Presbyterians to join the Anglican Church. The British wanted Charles Woodmason to convert the Carolina backwoodsmen to their Anglican religion. The Scots-Irish meeting houses often assembled one thousand parishioners most every Sunday in support of the Presbyterian ministry's fiery sermons against King George.

On one occasion, Woodmason was preaching when a gang of Presbyterians started whooping like a bunch of Indians on a war path. They hired a group of back woodsmen to bring over fifty dogs to church. When Woodmason started preaching, these back woodsmen set their dogs to fighting. Woodmason was petrified stating, "There is no possible way to charge these ruffians with a warrant. If I possibly served a warrant, the guards would obviously allow these Scots- Irish ruffians to escape."

To King George's disappointment, Anglican minister Woodmason was most un-welcome in the Scots-Irish backcountry. Obviously, he was not successful in converting these Presbyterian Carolina back woodsmen to the Crown's Anglican religion.

. Colonial dissention against the forced Anglican religion, with unjust tithes, reached a breaking point, especially in Virginia. Led by Patrick Henry, Virginia made loud outcries against the Crown's tithes. Henry joined forces with George Mason and Thomas Jefferson in Virginia's struggles for religious freedom. Actions of Virginia legislators leading up to the war limited the Anglican Church's political advantages. However, it was not until Virginia's General Assembly, in 1786, guaranteed freedom of religion under Jefferson's sponsored "Statute for Religious Freedom" that Virginia obtained freedom of religion.

The British accused the Presbyterian ministers of preaching rebellion from the pulpit. Many of the ministers and Presbyterian leaders became British targets. The Presbyterians, with their large congregations and renowned ministers preaching so vehemently for freedom and justice, were instrumental in winning America's Independence. In the western North Carolina countryside, the Presbyterians built their many community-meeting houses that served as their house of worship. In Caswell County, after leaving Duplin's Grove, Minister McAden preached at the Red House Church. The British during their Guilford campaign burned his home. Minister Patillo taught in Orange County, North Carolina where he led a campaign for freedom along the Eno River. In Guilford County, Reverend Caldwell ran a classical school and seminary where he provided support for independence from England.

In Rowan County, the scholarly Samuel McCorkle preached and taught many students. McCorkle became the first professor, when the doors of the nation's first public University opened in Chapel Hill. A number of his Rowan students joined him at the University.

In Iredell County, a Reverend Hall preached fiery sermons supporting America's independence. Reverend Hall led a number of men from his congregation onto the battlefield. Alexander Craighead, in Charlotte, preached a raging campaign of Independence from the pulpit and played an instrumental role when the brave Scots-Irish wrote and signed North Carolina's most famous

Mecklenburg Declaration, America's first signed Declaration for Independence.

Many of these brave Presbyterian ministers in the Carolina countryside vigorously led the Patriot's Revolutionary War for Independence. Reverend David Caldwell feverously preached against the torment of the British led by Cornwallis, especially at the time of the battles of Cowpens and Guilford Courthouse. The British, in retaliation, offered a large bounty for the minister's head. (Reference Presbyterian Minister William Foote's 1846 "Sketches of North Carolina" which describes the British placement of bounties on men of the cloth.) Despite their personal danger , many Presbyterian ministers played a key role in inspiring their parishioners to fight for freedom.

None of these ministers left their ministry, nor faltered in their Patriotic spirit, during the war. Their Presbyterian congregations were brave and heroic when their very families and homes were in danger. The Presbyterian courage was ingrained for over two and a half centuries in fighting the English Crown over religious and political liberty. They had endured the many murderous acts of the Stuart Kings, including King James II's horrific siege of Derry, where many faithful died of starvation. With America's victory at Yorktown, the freedom loving Presbyterians who persevered centuries of suffering could now proudly claim a lead role in gaining America's Freedom. These proud Scots-Irish Puritans were truly now **"FREE".**

With their British Commander Ferguson killed in their stunning loss to the Scots-Irish at Kings Mountain, the Loyalists limped from the battlefield causing Cornwallis to swear, "These villains, so called Presbyterians, have to be taught a lesson. I am immediately ordering my troops to burn their meeting-house churches where these Whig scoundrels meet to plan attacks on my British soldiers and our encampments."

British General Tarleton, "the Beast", in his memoirs of his Southern campaign through 1780-81, admitted to the burning of a number of churches including that of the Waxhaw Scots-Irish settlement. Tarleton declared all Presbyterian Churches to be shops of evil. However, it was the young Bannister Tarleton who refused granting quarter to revolutionary soldiers who had dropped their weapons in surrender at the Battle of Cowpens.

A Loyalist named Captain Huck joined in the British fight against the Scots -Irish back woodsmen of South Carolina. Prior to the war Captain Huck was a prominent lawyer in Philadelphia. In 1780 Huck sided with the Loyalists and followed Cornwallis and Tarleton to the western Carolinas. Huck disliked the Scots-Irish Presbyterians and made many raids on their churches and homes of their ministers. The Scots-Irish back-woodsmen in revenge finally killed Huck in York County, South Carolina. In July 1780 Cornwallis reported to his superior, Lord Clinton, that the Ulster, Carolina Scots-Irish, rebels killed Captain Huck. These Scots- Irish rebels showed no mercy for Huck's men and killed most of them. These back woodsmen's revenge on Captain Christian Huck helped spark a series of victories. The battle of Kings Mountain was won in October 1780, followed by David Morgan's victory at Cowpens, in 1781.

Following the Scots-Irish's vicious fighting in Carolina's battles of King's Mountain followed by Cowpens, Cornwallis wrote his superior, Lord Clinton, "The American Revolution is truly the Presbyterian's rebellious war." The battle of Guilford Courthouse proved even more to Cornwallis and King George that the war was truly a Presbyterian rebellion.

The major outcry during the war against the English crown was not from New England Puritans, nor New York Germans and Dutch, nor Virginia planters; but the "Scots-Irish Presbyterians". The Scots-Irish, with their huge rebellious outcry, anxiously awaited their revenge on English authority for the many years of slaughter and torture inflicted by the Crown on their ancestors. They so vividly remembered with much hatred the slaughter of their Scottish ancestors by the cruel Stuart Kings, Charles I and II and James I and II.

PART VI- The Founding of A NEW NATION
(1781-1805)

Following the war, the new nation, governed by the Articles of Confederation, was faced with drafting a Constitution that would ensure liberty and freedom for all. With the election of Washington as President, partisan battles raged between the Federalists and Anti-Federalists. There was much concern that the Constitution, influenced by the northern merchants, ignored the needs of the common man, especially the Scots-Irish laymen and farmers. North Carolina's Scots-Irish legislators demanded a "Bill of Rights" before ratifying the Constitution to become the twelfth state of the union. Battles continued to rage between the merchant supported Federalists and the more agrarian Anti-Federalists when the Jay Treaty was passed.

Following victory over Britain, North Carolina confiscated much of the un-granted land, the land of Tories, and the vast acreage granted to Henry McCulloch. The Scots-Irish were pleased to be rid of McCulloch, the Crown's crooked and swindling land speculator.

Alexandria Martin arranged to have a portion of the confiscated land set aside to support the nation's first new public university to enroll students. The University of North Carolina (UNC) colors represent the Blue and the Blue and White of Scotland's flag. David Gillespie, the son of Revolutionary hero James Gillespie, was the President of the first class of 1795 of the nation's first public University (UNC). David received an honorary scholastic certificate signed by Governor Samuel Ashe when he unselfishly sacrificed his college education to serve as surveyor under the "Treaty of San Lorenzo" to resolve America's territorial disputes with Spain.

The early years of the University were deeply

divided between Federalists and Anti-Federalists instructors, administrators, and trustees over University policy issues, including the passage of the Jay Treaty that provided certain war reparations for Tories. North Carolina Governor Davie, a Federalist, did not invite Governor Alexander Martin, an Anti-Federalists and President of the Board of Trustees for UNC, to his grandeur mason sponsored cornerstone laying ceremony.

Chapter 17
The Scots-Irish Presbyterian Clan of Duplin's Village of Grove

Dr. Herring, through his vast knowledge of the early history of Duplin County, the home of Congressman James Gillespie, provided insight into the heroic role of the County's Scots-Irish in North Carolina's battles to win freedom from England's yoke. Dr. Herring ranks with North Carolina's most knowledgeable and passionate historians. When he died in 2007, North Carolina, so sadly, lost its champion for junior colleges and Duplin and Sampson Counties lost their pioneering historian.

Many of the Pearsall's, Dickson's, Routledge's and Stalling's sons and daughters married within Congressman James Gillespie's family. Colonel Routledge's son, Thomas Routledge II, married Mildred Gillespie James youngest daughter. Following the war, Colonel Routledge served as sheriff of Duplin for many years and acted as chairman of the County Court.

Dr. David Gillespie was the grandson of James and the son of Joseph Gillespie. Dr. Gillespie first married Feribee Pearsall and upon her death, he married her sister Lucy Jane Pearsall. Robert Dickson, William Dickson's brother and close friend of the Gillespie family for many years, notarized Doctor Gillespie's marriage certificate. In early 1840, Dr. Gillespie and Lucy Jane built their two story Colonial home on today's Seminary Street near her father's famous Pearsall Spring. Their elegant home exemplifies Greek Revival architecture with peaked and crossetted windows and doors. This Greek Revival architecture was stylish in the 19th century Carolina southern plantation homes.

"Dr. David Gillespie and wife Lucy Jane Pearsall's home"

Feribee and Lucy Jane were the daughters of Sheriff James Pearsall, a colonel in the revolutionary war. James Pearsall owned the property where today's Kenansville Courthouse, the Grove Village's famous spring, and Dr. Gillespie's historic home are now located. He also owned and operated his very popular tavern, next door, where local gentry drank many stimulating spirits and socialized for many hours on end.

Clemont, oldest son of Joseph Gillespie, inherited the Gillespie Marsh Creek plantation and married Mary Pearsall. James Pearsall in 1780 donated four acres of land and his popular fresh water spring to the County of Duplin as a building site for the new courthouse. For his generosity, Duplin County allowed Pearsall to operate a tavern in his home next door to the Courthouse. With the courthouse next door, Pearsall's tavern served spirits and was a fashionable and popular gathering place. The Pearsall tavern provided much merriment for the local gents as well as a few ladies. The tavern served as a center to discuss local, state and federal politics.

The State Senate election of 1791, between Congressman Gillespie and General James Kenan, was a hot political topic argued for days on end by the Grove's Scots-Irish clan at the tavern over many glasses of rum and ale. Pearsall brought to his tavern excellent English rum and ale, especially for jubilant Scots-Irish victorious gatherings and celebrated occasions. One such event was the celebration of the 1800 election of Thomas Jefferson as the first Anti-Federalist president.

Another popular topic discussed at Pearsall's tavern was the crooked land grant scheme uncovered by Congressman James Gillespie and his colleagues during the late 1780's to early 1790's.

Colonel William Dickson's daughter, Susannah, married Congressman James' adopted son, Joseph. Upon her death, Joseph married Jane Stallings. Colonel William Dickson's son Joseph married Lucy Gillespie. Colonel Dickson who wrote the early history of Duplin's Grove, and Edward Pearsall were executors of Congressman Gillespie's estate upon his death in 1805.

Congressman Gillespie in his will provided for Charlotte and Joseph (Mumford) Gillespie his two adopted children who were his wife's brother's two children. Following the death of Dorcuses' brother, James Gillespie adopted and treated Charlotte and Joseph as loving members of their large close-knit Scots- Irish extended family.

James Gillespie willed Charlotte a feather bed and other furniture. James left Joseph his marsh creek plantation and a special silver Gillespie family watch brought over from Ulster. James displayed his love for Charlotte and Joseph in his will stating, "My beloved Mumford children are forever a part of my Gillespie family."

Charlotte went on to marry a Mr. Blaine a close relative of the renowned political leader James Gillespie Blaine of Maine. Joseph inherited much of James Gillespie's Tennessee military grant land along the beautiful Duck River in what is today's Maury County.

The Scots-Irish that settled in Duplin's Village Grove, like many others that settled all across America, retained the born-fighting spirit and close social bonding customs of their homeland Scotland. Over the centuries these Scots-Irish retained their values-based combativeness with refusal to be dominated by authoritarian rulers from above, regardless of the personal cost.

With their born -fighting spirit the men did not hesitate to volunteer to be a member of the Patriots' local militia. The continual battles of the Scots-Irish in Ireland and Scotland had hardened their entire family to face continual hardships. Their wives understood that they had a family duty to run all household affairs. This included their farm to ensure that food was available for family members when their husbands were away defending against Indian and British attacks.

These Grove Scots-Irish families had known forefathers in Scotland and Ireland. They had suffered together from the many evils of the Papist English Kings. Many had sailed together from Ulster sharing the many hardships as they crossed the Atlantic to America. They pooled their energies in meeting their living needs in everything from building their homes for shelter, their meeting house- Grove Church, and barn raisings to shelter their life essential farm animals.

Other traits included fostering and marriage alliances. In Duplin County when a husband and wife died and left children, the court assigned guardians for the orphans. Such an example was when General James Kenan's youngest daughter Catherine died, the Court appointed James Gillespie and James Kenan, on April 24,

1788, as guardians for her orphan children.

The Scots-Irish Village Grove families maintained close marriage alliances. Under a marriage contract, the groom often received livestock, slaves, and a dowry. At the outbreak of the Revolutionary war, the tightly knit Scots-Irish, with their born- fighting spirit, easily rallied their gentry to arms. Over the centuries, their kinsmen had joined the ongoing struggles against the English Crown.

Chapter 18
Post War Land Settlements in North Carolina

Following the Revolutionary War, the state of North Carolina confiscated all of the un-granted land, all the land of Henry McCulloch as well as much of the Carolina land owned by the Tories who had fled the country. In 1778, the state began new land grants under laws structured to correct proprietor evils such as defective grants, land swindles and fraud. Despite North Carolina's appointment of commissioners to correct land deed problems and prevent swindles, the land thieves exercised a new creative form of land theft. The new laws specified that the first entry was to take precedence over that of all others. The complicated problem that allowed swindles under the "first entry" law was the absence of deed records due to fire, military destruction and inaccurate record keeping.

An unscrupulous individual, through a "prior entry" scheme, swindled Benjamin Cleveland, the heroic Colonial Commander for the battle of King's Mountain, of his plantation. He lost his property in Wilkes County called "Roundabout". Joel Lewis used the" prior entry" scheme to steal Cleveland's Roundabout plantation house and land. Cleveland lost his court appeal and in disgust moved to South Carolina.

In Guildford County, the appointed land Commissioners divided confiscated land for auction into carefully rigged sales. The clerk of court Thomas Henderson and Governor Alexander Martin bought Guildford Courthouse and a large tract of land adjacent to the courthouse land. They divided the land into town lots they sold over the years. Henderson and Martin renamed this Courthouse land "Martinville".

Military Land Grants

In 1782 North Carolina established a land reservation to pay their Revolutionary Soldiers and to support a militia for their new State government. State officials appointed Colonel Martin Armstrong as North Carolina's entry recorder and chief surveyor for the military grants. North Carolina's Secretary of State, James Glasgow, issued the military grants, assigning each a warrant number. After North Carolina Secretary of State James Glasgow assigned an eligible soldier a land warrant, the soldier selected a specific location within the military reservation. The rectangular shaped reservation was in the Cumberland River Valley. The reservation began on the Tennessee River and ran 55 miles to the south, then 130 miles east, then 55 miles north.

James Gillespie chose a number of locations for his military grants within this Cumberland River Valley military reservation. Among the grants entered and issued were:

- 3030 acres on the Duck River: entered 1783, Issued 1792 (James gave his orphaned and adopted son, Joseph "Mumford" Gillespie much of his Duck River Property.)
- 640 acres on the south side of Little River: Issued Feb 4, 1795
- Lick Creek: Entered 1783 and Issued 1787
- 640 acres north side of Cumberland River waters of Big Barron
- James Gillespie received Cornelius Ryan's Cumberland Valley War Warrant: Entered 1791 and Issued 1793.

James gave a majority of his Tennessee land to his adopted son Joseph. Joseph's descendants settled in Mt Pleasant, Jacks Creek, Columbia and several other towns along the Cumberland Valley of Tennessee.

In the fall of 1796, Tennessee's newly elected Congressman Andrew Jackson discovered through his Tennessee associates and his brother in- law Donaldson, that many prominent Tennessee men were deeply involved in the fraudulent land warrant schemes, especially Donaldson. Through North Carolina land officials, with control of land documents, these crooks orchestrated many schemes to steal vast amounts of military grant lands. Jackson discovered that a leader of the land warrant forgeries was none other than his arch political rival Governor Sevier. Sevier, a war hero at Kings Mountain, was held with high esteem in Western North Carolina and East Tennessee. Anxiously, Jackson sought support from Senator Alexandria Martin and Congressman James Gillespie, and in turn Governor Ashe. Jackson wrote an affidavit letter to Governor Ashe setting forth evidence of the Tennessee land fraud activity.

Assessing the evidence, Governor Ashe requested that the North Carolina legislature investigate the alleged land fraud. The North Carolina government's inquiry uncovered numerous fraudulent schemes and falsification of courthouse land records.

The investigation discovered that Colonel Martin Armstrong amassed over 260,000 acres of land by means of erroneous grants through which he and his brother, John, fraudulently seized many thousands of acres. Stokely Donaldson and William Terrell stole over ½ million acres. Terrell was the son-in-law of James Glasgow the North Carolina's Secretary of State. Glasgow embossed his signature on the many grants of his son in law. The fraudulent schemes used by Armstrong, the principal surveyor, included issuing land grants to non-soldiers, duplicate warrants, and forged signatures. North Carolina's military land grant fiasco was known as the "Glasgow Land Fraud". It was named for Secretary of State Glasgow the ring leader of the State's fraudulent schemes. Glasgow was highly respected as a Revolutionary War hero and considered as especially loyal to North Carolina prior to discovery of his leading role in the North Carolina's massive land fraud operation. Governor Ashe often referred to Glasgow as North Carolina's "Fallen Angel".

Governor Ashe aggressively pursued prosecution of those involved in the land frauds. However, when William Davie replaced Ashe as Governor, he lacked zeal in pursuing the prosecution of those involved. Davie as Governor sought little punishment for those involved in the fraudulent land schemes. Federalists Party members were associated with the majority of the land frauds.

Duplin war heroes including William Dickson, James Pearsall and Colonel Routledge honorably received a number of military land grants in the Cumberland Valley military reservation. Colonel William Dickson gave over six hundred acres of his military grant land to his son William who was a graduate of the Duplin Grove Academy. William Dickson became a doctor and eventually a Congressman from Tennessee. Tennessee named Dickson County for Congressman Dickson. James Gillespie gave much of his Tennessee land grants on Little River, Duck River and Lick Creek, in what is now Maury County Tennessee to his son Joseph.

Gillespie's Duplin Land Holdings

In December 1770, Josiah Martin was selected by King George III to replace the very unpopular and corrupt Governor Tryon. To ease the ill feeling of North Carolina citizens toward Tryon's unscrupulous land dealings, especially in Alamance County, Governor Josiah Martin established a land patent office. During this period from 1770 through 1775, James Gillespie successfully obtained a number of land patents from Governor Martin. Combined with his land Patents from Governor Martin and his various land purchases and state grants from confiscated Tory land, Gillespie's land holdings in the Duplin County countryside totaled over 4000 acres. His land holdings included property on Marsh Creek, Maxwell Branch, Limestone Branch, and Dark Branch. The census for that time indicates Gillespie was one of the larger local slave owners with over thirty slaves. Musician Dizzy Gillespie is a descendent of slaves owned by the Gillespies.

Following the Redcoats burning of the Gillespie plantation, James moved his family to his new home North East of today's Kenansville. The site of his rebuilt plantation, Golden Grove, can be found by traveling North East from Kenansville, N. C. on Route 11. Drive past the property he obtained from minister McAden and turn right onto SR-1900, travel about two miles and turn right onto Earl Davis Farm Road. Unfortunately, today there are few ruins remaining of Congressman Gillespie's plantation which was within site of the family's cemetery, referred to today as the Joseph Gillespie family cemetery. Joseph, a North Carolina State Senator, was the adopted son of Congressman Gillespie. He inherited his father, Congressman Gillespie's, home-site. Joseph in his June 1835 will deeded the Marsh Creek Gillespie homestead to his son Clemont. Joseph Gillespie and members of his family are buried in the Gillespie family Cemetery.

Grave Stone of Joseph Gillespie (Congressman Gillespie's adopted son)- Located in Gillespie Cemetery

James Gillespie and family produced large quantities of tar, pitch and turpentine rendered from their numerous long leaf pine trees on their Elder, Limestone and Maxwell swamp properties along the Northeast Cape Fear River. The Gillespies and other Duplin families sold their naval store products through the port of Wilmington. The tar, pitch and turpentine from Carolina's numerous pine trees were vital to the marine industry. The Colonials used tar for axle grease and for machinery lubrication, pitch to seal wooden boat hulls as watertight, turpentine for paint thinner and linseed oil for medicinal purposes. The Gillespies, joined by other Duplin landowners, floated their huge casks of tar pitch and barrels of turpentine on log rafts down the Northeast Cape Fear River to market in Wilmington.

Duplin's families ferried back many household staple goods especially barrels of salt that were evaporated from salt stills at the Ocean's edge to their plantations. The James Gillespie family operated a large gristmill at the 15-mile post on the Northeast Cape Fear River for grinding corn and wheat into meal and flour.

Chapter 19
Duplin County's Civic and Legislative Affairs

James Gillespie played an integral role in the legislative affairs of Duplin County, North Carolina, as well as State and Federal legislative affairs. At the time of his membership in North Carolina's Fifth Provincial Congress of 1776, James aided in the writing of North Carolina's Constitution and ensured the assembly included provisions for the protection of the common man. Through the support of his many Scots- Irish colleagues, the State's Constitution was easily ratified. North Carolina followed closely the drafting of the new nation's Declaration and Constitution as well as the efforts of Thomas Jefferson relative to the Virginia State Legislature. One of the key writings James Gillespie and his colleagues referenced was Thomas Jefferson's 1774 manuscript written for Virginia's Williamsburg State Constitutional delegation entitled "Summary of the Rights of British America". Today, James Gillespie's copy of this famous Jefferson writing of 1774 is cataloged in Duke University's Devil's Den Library.

The North Carolina Constitution reflects the distrust that the Scots-Irishmen had for "executive power". The North Carolina Constitution was drafted by the many Scots-Irishmen who insisted that their state Governor be allowed only a one year term and within six years only three terms. The Constitution mandated a seven man, "Council of State" panel to oversee the Governor to ensure that the use of his executive power was not abusive. It wasn't until the late 20th century that the N. C. legislature authorized a gubernatorial second term and veto over proposed legislation.

Other legislation drafted by Gillespie and his contemporaries during their Halifax assembly included the Governor's power to appoint justices to hold the County Courts of Pleas and Quarter sessions. The County Court held sessions four times a year for a week usually January, April, July and October. From 1777 through 1782, James Gillespie, William Dickson, James Pearsall, and Tom Routledge from the Village of Grove, and James Kenan from the local community of Turkey served as Justices of the Peace for Duplin County.

The Justices were empowered to conduct the following matters including:

> *Issue licenses for taverns and the setting of prices for store goods, food, and drinks
> *Enforce wills and deeds after a petitioner signed a will or deed, when he appeared in open court to swear as to its authenticity prior to the recording of the document.
> *Issue and sign marriage bonds for white people to marry
> (During the 1700's Negroes were not allowed to marry legally.)
> *Oversee the maintenance and construction of roads and bridges and to approve tolls for roads and bridges with fees to be posted.
> *Conduct criminal trials and enter judgments

(On Thursday March 15, 1787, Duplin's Justices of the Peace, Gillespie, Kenan, Dickson and Pearsall presided over a famous trial of two Negro slaves, Darby and Peter. The two slaves belonged to Colonel William Taylor. Darby, a middle aged Negro man, confessed to the murder with an axe of his Master Taylor. Darby, during an argument with his master, viciously struck his Master Taylor in the head with the weapon and instantly killed him. The court's death sentence read: "The said Negro Darby, he is given to God under guard and tomorrow between hours of one and four o'clock in the afternoon, he will be tied to stake on the courthouse lot, and burned to ashes with ashes strewn across the ground."

Duplin's jail man dragged accomplice Peter, the twelve year old slave, viciously onto the courthouse lawn, cut one-half of each ear off, lashed the bound and scared negro boy one hundred times and branded each of his cheeks with "M" for murderer.)

Today, the North Carolina State Archives maintains a file of the Village of Grove, Duplin Court records from the court sessions, beginning in 1784, over which James Gillespie presided. Unfortunately, no court records remain for Duplin's first courthouse located along Turkey Branch. The Turkey Branch Court held sessions from 1750 through 1784. Fortunately, the Sampson County Courthouse maintains a file consisting of eight books of land deeds and slave bills of sale for the early Turkey Branch, Duplin County Court. Sampson County was established from the western part of Duplin.

Other duties and responsibilities assigned to Duplin's justices were overseeing the assignment of orphans to responsible families until each child reached twenty-one years of age. One such assignment, assigned to Gillespie as justice, involved the orphans of Thomas Kenan's daughter. Other justice duties were issuance of permits for boat docks, gristmills, and guns in addition to the election of the Sheriff and County Tax and County Tax Assessor.

The Justices of Peace remained the local governing body of North Carolina Counties until 1868 when County

Commissioners became the governing authority for County finances. Today, state paid personnel manage all of the county court administrative duties for the State of North Carolina.

Chapter 20
James Gillespie's North Carolina Legislative Service

In order to prevent more conflicts with the State's colonial Governor, Josiah Martin, that were frequent, the colony of North Carolina elected a Provincial Congress independent to that of their colonial governor. The N. C. Patriots held five consecutive provincial legislatures. Their Fifth Congress of 1776 wrote and ratified the North Carolina Constitution. These Constitutional Delegates established their State General Assembly as North Carolina's ruling arm. The General Assembly was composed of the State Senate and House of Commons elected by the populous. Each County had one Senator and two House of Commons delegates. Qualifying towns were allowed to elect one House of Commons delegate. Only land owning Protestants, mostly Scots-Irish Presbyterians, were allowed to serve in the North Carolina legislature. These legislators long remembered the Papist and Anglican Rogues, especially during the reign of the Stuart Kings.

All too familiar with the abuse from the executive power of the British Crown, the General Assembly appointed the Governor for a term of only one year. The Governor was only allowed three terms within six years. With justification, the Assembly could remove the Governor.

To provide additional control over executive power, a seven man "Council of State" was selected by the General Assembly that effectively controlled the Governor's decisions. The Governor was required to seek the Council's advice and consent on all-important matters. These Carolina legislators recalled Benjamin Franklin's remark during the drafting of the "Articles of Confederation", "To control the dangers of executive power possibly the office of Presidency should be held by a select panel of elected men in lieu of one man"

James Gillespie served in North Carolina's House of Commons during and after the Revolutionary war. In 1788, Gillespie was elected as a state Senator to serve on the prestigious seven man "Council of State". Under Governor Martin, James Gillespie with other Council of State members were influential during the 1789 Fayetteville Constitutional Assembly. These Council of State members guided Governor Martin in the challenging decision for North Carolina to ratify the U. S. Constitution. Charles Rodenbough, in his biography of "Governor Alexander Martin", depicts the difficult task with which Martin was confronted in persuading the legislators to ratify the U.S. Constitution to allow North Carolina to become the 12th state to the Union.

Gillespies' House of Commons service was followed by five terms as a state senator. Following his State Senatorial service, James Gillespie served over a decade as a U.S. Congressman beginning in Philadelphia in 1793.

As a legislator, James was attentive, decisive, somewhat reserved, and polite by nature. His legislative colleagues appointed Gillespie to many important committee positions addressing difficult and complex problems.

In the U.S. Congress, James served diligently with much proficiency. His very low-key and untiring service was reflected on numerous state house and senatorial committees, James lived by the Gillespie family motto "to be rather than to seem". Recognizing the merits of this motto, North Carolina, in 1893, adopted the Gillespie family motto "Esse Quam Videri" which is Latin for "to be rather than to seem" as the North Carolina motto.

James Gillespie's legislative service during the last twenty five years of the 18th century, ranks near the top in achievement and consistency with his political compatriots Martin, Caswell, Johnson, Hawkins, Bloodworth, Macon, and Williamson for holding major North Carolina governmental offices. Gillespie's legislative service for North Carolina was impeccable. He served almost continuously as a state and federal office holder from 1776 until his death while in the U. S. Congress in 1805.

Beginning in 1776, James was a member of the 1776 Halifax Provincial Congress which ratified the North Carolina Constitution. James along with other Scots-Irishmen, such as Waightsville Avery, insisted on key educational language to support a new State University. James, along with Richard Clinton, represented Duplin County in the State House of Commons from 1779 to1784.

These were bitter years during and after the Revolutionary War. The House of Commons legislators, during these dangerous times of the British and Tories overrunning their countryside, met at three locations Smithfield, Halifax and New Bern. During his early service in the House of Commons, Gillespie won the friendship and admiration of many state legislators, including Bloodworth, Macon, Martin, Mathew Locke, Nathan Bryan, and Absalom Tatum.

In 1778, Gillespie was appointed as committee chairman to consolidate the towns of Campbeltown and Cross-Creek into the incorporated town of Fayetteville. North Carolina named Fayetteville to honor Marquis de Lafayette and his revolutionary war services to George Washington's army. North Carolina's state legislature named Main Street, running north and south through the old market square, Gillespie Street to honor James Gillespie for his expert surveying service in laying out the streets of Fayetteville and his heroic, faithful, revolutionary service to North Carolina and to America.

Fayetteville, situated at the head waters of the Cape Fear River, provided valuable colonial inland water transportation to the state's deep-water port of Wilmington. Soon, Fayetteville became a flourishing commercial center.

On November 19, 1786, Governor Richard Caswell, at the General Assembly held in New Bern, appointed James Gillespie to the North Carolina Militia State Committee. His first committee assignment was preparing a bill to reestablish militia authority for North Carolina. The bill set forth the command structure and approved provisions including horse, saddle and boots. It authorized pay for the militia according to respective rank.

The State Senate appointed three formal generals of the militia, including James Gillespie, to organize North Carolina's troops to protect the state. Following the Revolutionary War, the new nation had continuing concerns for possible attacks from England, Spain, and France, not to mention the ever-threatening raids of Indians along the frontier.

Similarly in the early 1800's, shortly after Tennessee became a state, Andrew Jackson was selected to head up the Tennessee State militia. Obviously, Jackson's militia duties became much more famous in history than those of Gillespie's resulting in Jackson's winning the Battle of New Orleans with his Tennessee mountain men of mostly Scots-Irish ruffians. Although the battle occurred after the Treaty officially ending the War of 1812, this victory boosted the national exposure of Andrew Jackson to run for president of the United States as the first Scots-Irishman.

James Gillespie served in the State House of Commons, along with Timothy Bloodworth. The two co-authored a bill in 1784 to repeal North Carolina laws which supported repayment of British Loyalist losses as specified by the 1783 Paris Peace Treaty with England. Gillespie was furious that Jay and Adams showed partiality to Britain during the Paris Peace Treaty negotiations. Adams and Jay, during the Paris peace conferences, agreed to repay the British Loyalists for their confiscated land and burned homes. Fortunately, for America, Benjamin Franklin opposed full repayment. He persuaded the British to accept truce terms that any Loyalist who raised arms against the revolutionaries was not to be compensated.

In 1791 James Gillespie ran against James Kenan from Turkey, Dublin County for the North Carolina Senate. Under oath, Gillespie disputed his unfavorable N. C. State Senate election results.

William Dickson, Clerk of Duplin Court, signed and submitted Gillespie's sworn affidavit to the State Assembly setting forth evidence that Gillespie received a majority of lawful votes. Supporting the voting dispute were a number of voting affidavits indicating that Sheriff David Glisson conducted the election improperly. To vote, a voter was required to show ownership of property. After Kenan reviewed the notarized voter information, he resigned from the election of 1791. Thus, Gillespie was elected to serve his 5th term in the North Carolina State Senate.

Earlier in September 1781, following Fannon's capture of Governor Burke, Alexander Martin became acting Governor for North Carolina. Martin immediately called upon his trusted ,Scots-Irish compatriot, Gillespie with his unusually keen intellectual ability and bravery, to assist him in his administrative duties as Governor.

In September 1781 with the British and Tories overrunning the Carolina countryside, the State's Governorship was in chaos and crisis. Governor Martin to prevent capture was constantly on the move holding State legislative meetings at three different locations.

A large trunk of legislative papers had to be continuously moved without being stolen. With Governor Burke in British hands and imprisoned on Ellis Island, and the British and Loyalist militia overrunning the countryside, North Carolina was in an extreme state of emergency.

An important assignment for the Governor's office

was drafting a letter for Martin's signature to British Major Craig requesting release of Burke. Craig refused and viewed Burke as too valuable a prisoner to release. Craig realized how valuable the captured North Carolina Patriot Governor was for future war negotiations.

Governor Martin received requests from Nathaniel Greene through General Rutherford, recently appointed as head of North Carolina's militia, to order and supply all available weapons and ammunition possible and approve the mustering of all available troops for an immediate attack on Wilmington. General Washington had informed Greene that Wilmington must be re-taken and the control of the port was critical to winning the war and negotiating peace. Martin, with the aid of Gillespie, mustered as many troops as possible to advance a Patriot attack on Wilmington.

On October 23, 1781, acting Governor Martin, supported by Major James Gillespie and a contingent of Whig militia, met with General Rutherford at Brown Marsh, just southeast of Elizabethtown. Rutherford briefed Martin on the Patriot strategy to free Wilmington from British control.

General Rutherford, during his advance on Wilmington, attacked the Tories with hatred and vengeance. Much animosity was instilled from his Rowan County plantation being ransacked earlier by the British. In addition, Rutherford was wounded and captured due to Gates' disastrous command over the Battle of Camden.

Rutherford's attack strategy was to advance on Wilmington from both sides of the Cape Fear River. Rutherford led a Whig attack down the North East, Heron Bridge, side of the Cape Fear River, while Captain Robert Smith led a Patriot cavalry down the South East shore on the Livingston Creek side of the Cape Fear, River. During the first part of November the Patriots fought skirmishes in their advance on Wilmington. On November 16th, Lt.

Colonel Light Horse Lee jubilantly rode into Rutherford's Heron Bridge campsite with the victorious news that Cornwallis had surrendered at Yorktown on October 19, 1781. During the next few days Rutherford's militia, riding victoriously into Wilmington, drove the British aboard sailing vessels and out to sea. It had been five long years since the residents of the lower Cape Fear had declared war against the Crown and their Loyalist's neighbors.

Alexander Martin and Congressman Gillespie over the years were faithful political allies, especially during their joint service in the 1785 North Carolina State senate in which Martin was appointed Speaker. Martin and Gillespie remained close friends, over the late 1700s, as confirmed by their correspondence that is catalogued at the Library of Congress.

Martin, North Carolina's Governor from 1782-1784 and 1789-1792, was the son of Hugh Martin from County Tyrone, Ireland who was a Scots-Irish Presbyterian minister. Martin was a graduate of the New Jersey Seminary that became Princeton University.

Martin served in Congress with Gillespie, Martin a Senator and James Gillespie a Congressman. They were elected to the Fourth and Fifth Congresses. Martin, to the disappointment of Gillespie, leaned toward the Federalists and supported Adams for President, and voted for the Alien and Sedition Act. Shortly thereafter, Gillespie and his Jeffersonian compatriots organized North Carolina's Warren Junta Club whose members nominated Jefferson in the Presidential Caucus of 1800.

Governor Martin and James Gillespie over the years provided much support to North Carolina and America's first public state University. They supported state legislature to obtain confiscated land that would, upon sale, provide funds for the new University. The University's Board of Trustees, in 1790, elected Martin to serve as their first President. Martin served as the University Board of

Trustee President until his death in 1807.

Rodenbough, in his biography of Alexander Martin, discussed how Martin furthered education in North Carolina. Martin's family held education in high esteem, perhaps even higher than the typical Scots-Irish Presbyterian with their many log cabin schools which laid the foundation for America's educational system.

In 1783, the first academy west of the Alleghany's was named for Governor Martin due to his huge support of education in North Carolina. A few years later, Governor Martin sponsored an educational bill, in 1788, which established an academy in Salisbury. It was called Liberty Hall and was named after the Queens academy where the Mecklenburg Resolve was drafted and signed. The Queens/ Mecklenburg Academy closed due to the Revolutionary War. During the war the academy served as a British hospital.

Ironically, when Martin's nemesis Davie organized the University of North Carolina's founding celebration, sponsored by the Masons, he conveniently forgot to invite Martin the President of the Board of Trustees. Anyway, Martin wasn't terribly disappointed since he at the time was receiving his honorary doctorate from Princeton University presented by Witherspoon.

Chapter 21
North Carolina's Scots-Irish Demand a Bill of Rights

James Gillespie served as a member of the second North Carolina Constitutional Assembly Convention of 1789 that met in Fayetteville on Gillespie Street, the street named in Congressman Gillespie's honor. The major legislative concern for the 1789 Constitutional Assembly was ratification of the U. S. Constitution and approval of a charter for the State's first public University. The State General Assembly elected Gillespie as a member of the seven man "Council of State" whose task was to assist, advise, and approve Governor Martin's many tough gubernatorial decisions during their many hours of meetings struggling over ratification issues. Of chief concern was incorporation of legislation to protect the common man from future abuses of the Federal Government; possible abuses similar to those imposed by the Stuart Kings through their "Kingly Rights".

The new nation recognized that problems existed with the "Articles of Confederation". The delegates considered individual freedom to be of the utmost importance in the Articles of Confederation. However, the Articles failed to give thorough consideration as to how the states were to operate as a union. The Articles failed to resolve many issues that crossed state borders.

Anti-Federalists James Gillespie, Timothy Bloodworth, Nathaniel Macon and Absalom Tatum, sought checks and balances over executive power. What should be the interface in the appointment of Supreme Court judges?

The Anti-Federalists continued to be concerned about Congress accepting responsibility for British war debts. At the Paris Peace Treaty negotiations Benjamin Franklin opposed the new nation's accepting any war debts. Jay and Adams disagreed. Fortunately Franklin added Treaty terms that those Loyalists bearing arms were not to be paid.

Franklin was concerned that the office of President possessed too much power. He stated, "Instead of one man possessing much executive power, possibly, a panel of executors is necessary to prevent abuse of power." In America's 21st century, issues of executive branch abuse of power continue today.

Gillespie and his colleagues worried over the treaty making power of the new federal Government. They did not want the Senate and President to approve treaties with other nations. They believed that the House of Representatives would best reflect the will of the electorate in treaty approval.

Governor Martin counselled with James Gillespie and other council members for many hours at Fayetteville's Cool Springs Tavern to discuss their concerns regarding ratification of the U.S. Constitution.

- -FAYETTEVILLE'S COOL SPRING TAVERN –

James Gillespie wanted a "Bill of Rights" in the U.S. Constitution to defend the individual rights of the common man. This was important to his constituency of

Scots-Irish farmers.

Gillespie and his Anti-Federalists allies, along with one Federalist delegate, refused to ratify America's Constitution without a Bill of Rights. A Bill of Rights was so dear to the 1789 North Carolina Assembly that met to ratify the U.S. Constitution. George Washington personally pleaded with the states, especially North Carolina that was undecided in their vote, to ratify the Constitution.

Earlier on June 12, 1776, George Mason, Patrick Henry and James Madison drafted as part of the Virginia State Constitution a Virginia Bill of Rights. Virginia's Bill of Rights guaranteed freedom of religion. It was in stark contrast to the centuries' old British practice of merging church and state.

In drafting the first twelve amendments for America's Constitution the Anti-federalists, led by Patrick Henry and supported by the North Carolina and Rhode Island assemblies, reminded the convention of Virginia's earlier State Bill of Right demands. Virginia's demands focused on religious freedom and Thomas Jefferson's Virginia Statute that finally provided Virginia's religious freedom.. Jefferson's statute was drafted in 1777, but wasn't enacted until 1786. The twelve amendments emphasized freedom of speech, **religion**, press and assembly. They included the right to petition the Government over grievances, the right of trial by jury and the guarantee of due process of law.

Of all of Jefferson's accomplishments, he stated that he was proudest of his Virginia Statute which ensured Virginia's religious freedom from the yoke of the Anglican Church. He insisted that his tombstone at Monticello be inscribed to indicate his religious freedom accomplishment.

Jefferson's Tombstone (inscribed with statute of Virginia's Religious Freedom) @ Monticello

Patrick Henry was raised by his mother, a devout Presbyterian. She raised Patrick Henry with devout Presbyterian doctrine principles in the rural countryside of Virginia. Henry became exceptionally popular with Virginia's freedom-loving Puritan Presbyterians as a young attorney by winning the famous Parsons Case in 1763. The Parson legal decision in favor of Virginia Presbyterians blocked the payment of tithes to the parsons of the Crown's aristocratic Episcopal Church of England. After the Parson case victory, colonial America viewed Patrick Henry as the leader for the protection of colonial religious freedom.

Many of Virginia's legislators were huge plantation

owners and staunch Anglicans and were Sovereign to the Crown. As legislators they forced the British Anglican Church and faith upon the populous. These aristocratic legislators were more than happy to collect the tithes for the Church, since in many cases they received bribes.

Patrick Henry, like many other Scots-Irishmen across colonial America, crusaded adamantly for the Constitution's Bill of Rights. Their ancestors in Ireland and Scotland were deprived for centuries of their individual freedom and liberties, thus, they were adamant that America be provided individual liberties through a "Bill of Rights".

Charles D. Rodenbough in his biography of "Governor Alexander Martin" describes how Martin with his political diplomacy and keen Princeton intellect led North Carolina to ratify the Constitution. Martin with Gillespie and the six other "council of state" advisers were faced with a monumental task to convince their adamant Anti-Federalists colleagues that it was imperative that North Carolina join the union and that their individual rights and liberties would be protected.

The Anti-Federalists delegates, including Bloodworth, Macon and Tatum faithfully supported the frontier farmers with their needs for individual rights and liberties. Martin, and his advisers, recognized the important consequence of North Carolina ratifying the U.S. Constitution to prevent any of the original thirteen colonies from breaking their unity as various British diplomats predicted.

Fortunately for North Carolina, James Gillespie, who so greatly feared excess executive power, and a number of other Anti-Federalists originally voting "nay", voted for ratification when they were assured the Constitution would later contain a Bill Of Rights.

Washington ordered fourteen ornate, gold framed, calfskin copies of the Bill of Rights signed by Vice

President John Adams and Speaker of the House Muhlenberg. Washington presented each of the thirteen states with its own copy of the Bill of Rights. Washington's personal efforts had greatly encouraged the North Carolina delegates to ratify the U.S. Constitution; thus, North Carolina became the 12th state to the union.

Meanwhile during this period with the assistance of his Federalists supporters, President Washington expanded his Presidential powers. These included power to send troops to war, authority to spend public monies , make foreign policy agreements and issue executive orders that carried force of law. These expanded Presidential powers were all without Constitutional sanctions or consent of Congress or the people.

Unbelievably, Sherman's' Union army, in 1865, usurped North Carolina's precious Bill of Rights freedom document out of the State Capital. For over 140 years, one antique dealer after the next traded and sold this pilfered and fragile calfskin document.

North Carolina's copy of the Bill of Rights traded several times, first in 1877 for five dollars, and again in 1995 for two hundred thousand dollars. When the FBI seized this stolen Bill of Rights, North Carolina finally had its precious freedom document for which James Gillespie and other North Carolina Scots-Irish Anti-Federalists had fought so long and hard. The State's legendary Bill of Rights copy is now preserved and cherished in North Carolina's Capitol.

Kenyon in her book entitled, "Men of Little Faith-the Anti- Federalists on the nature of Representative Government" labeled James Gillespie and his staunch North Carolina legislative colleagues as "Men of Little Faith". In truth, they had wisdom as to the dangers of abuse of federal power.

The Federalists referred to Gillespie and his Scots-Irish Republicans as "Anti-Democratic". These brave

Scots-Irishmen were the opposite. They represented the result of free democratic elections as reflective of the North Carolina Constitution. They were visionaries knowing from their ancestors' persecution by the English King's executive power the many dangers of "Acts of Legislative Tyranny".

Clearly, James Gillespie and his Democratic Republicans and Anti-Federalists colleagues were not men of little faith. They were courageous visionaries who understood the need for Constitutional protection against abusive actions of unscrupulous legislators, jurists and executives. The many centuries of horrific abuse inflicted by the British on the Scots-Irish provided an excellent understanding of the necessity for Constitutional protections and their enforcements. These laymen-farmers wanted foolproof safe-guards against any abuse of government power. They mandated explicit 5th Amendment due process requirements upon the federal government.

Kenyon's accusations were unfair and written without understanding and recognizing how these heroic Scots-Irishmen came off their farms and from the backwoods "whipping the devil" out of Generals Cornwallis and Tarleton in Carolina's battles to ensure **freedom** for America.

Carolina's Scots-Irish Patriots ensured democracy within their state by writing North Carolina's State Constitution that provided a House of Commons and State Senate with judiciary oversight concerning executive power. They helped structure the "Articles of Confederation" insisting on control over legislators. They knew that the "Articles of Confederation" were in need of improvement to resolve issues among the states. They did not wish to sacrifice their personal rights and liberty. They recognized, all too well, that the U. S. Constitution required language to protect the personal liberty and rights of all citizens.

These "Sons of Liberty, through their vision, knew all too well that metes and bounds ,firmly established controls, were an absolute necessity for America's Congress. They knew that certain Congressmen would become professional politicians with their primary objective being re-election. These colonial legislators knew the possibility of politicians misspending the public's hard-earned money with very little conscience to achieve their constituents' objectives. On the other hand, the Federalists to a large degree believed that the politicians, supported by the merchant aristocrats, knew best and should be allowed to operate the new republic with indirect democracy. However, it is obvious that the Federal government's legitimacy is truly based upon the consent of the governed.

To some extent America's **Bill of Rights,** achieved in part some of James Gillespie and his colleagues concerns relative to protecting the **rights and liberties** of the nation's citizens. These founding fathers, however, knew the Constitution needed definitive language to control the Federal Government, especially powers of the executive branch. How to select members of the Supreme Court other than choice by the President was of much concern.

They wanted specific institutional checks to guarantee individual **freedom.** With Washington's generous "Bill of Rights" platitude, however, most recognized no viable alternative was available other than to ratify the Constitution. Finally, James Gillespie in support of his longtime friend, Governor Martin, voted for ratifying the Constitution to the disappointment of many of his close colleagues. A number of other Anti-Federalists refused to vote for ratification. These "sons of liberty" wanted detailed provisions to protect the rights of citizens. A key Congressional control they desired was House of Representatives ratification of a treaty instead of the Senate. They were livid over the Paris Peace provisions that specified payment to the British and Loyalist for their war losses. Gillespie and his colleagues recommended several additional amendments. However, their Federal controls became impossible due to the strong objections of the Federalists. Gillespie, Macon, Locke, and other legislators sought protection for their individual rights but soon, in desperation, they gave up.

These freedom loving colonial Scots-Irish, Anti-Federalists, desired controls over Congressmen to prevent their putting their own self-interest before the interest of the common man whom they represented. Today, Gillespie and the other Anti-Federalists would be extremely concerned about America's limited control over the self serving legislators who up to recently could use inside information for stock trades.

Their foresight was excellent and today these "sons of liberty" would likely demand:

*Congressional term limits to control the establishment of Congressional lobby fraternities that ensure the Congressmen's re-election and payoffs by sole source contractors and Wall Street brokers.

-Our economic crisis of 2008 vividly illustrated how the Congress is being bought off by the lobbyists. Very little of the Dodd Frank "land mark financial reform" legislation to impose openness on Wall Street has been effective.

-In 2012 more than three quarters of the Dodd Frank reforms have not been approved due to the Wall Street Lobby spending more than $300 million dollars to kill rules for an equal playing field.

*That Wall Street not be allowed to gamble with the money of individual households, pension funds, mutual funds, university endowments and retirement funds. Wall Street does not gamble with the money of the rich.

-The players of Wall Street know both sides of the financial card of winners and losers.

-They know or have expectations of what rule changes will effect whom. Today's financial system is rigged against the ordinary system, in favor of the banks, which privatize the gains to an elite few with the downsized risks socialized to everyone.

-The six largest banks have grown from 20% to 60% control over the market since the financial meltdown.

*That Judges be held accountable for any corrupt or malicious act. Today in many cases, corrupt and malicious acts by judges are ignored claiming these judges are protected under absolute immunity.

-Colonial Patriots fought the revolution to escape the absolute tyrannical power of English Kings. Placing our Judges under absolute immunity, immune from our laws including financial disclosure, destroys the Constitution's doctrine of separation of power to provide checks and balances.

*That Congressmen's retirement pension must be in line with that of Federal Government employees. A full pension is available to members of Congress at age 62 with five years of service, 50 years or older with 20 years of service, or 25 years of service at any age. In retrospect a federal employee must work forty two years to receive a full pension today.

*That Congressman should not have the right to vote themselves substantial pay raises that apply immediately. Veteran preference is not enforced and often circumvented by the federal bureaucracy.

*That Congressmen's pay raises should be the same as the increases provided for America's social security system. (etc. CPI 3%). If Congress chooses not to provide citizens a social security increase, why should Congress receive an increase in their Congressional pay.

Many citizens in the 21st century have petitioned

Congress to pass the following proposed 28th Amendment to the Constitution and allow the States to vote on the Amendment for acceptance into our nation's Constitution.

"Congress shall make no law that applies to any citizen of the United States that does not apply equally to Congress, both house and Senate. Congress shall make no law that applies to any U. S. Senator or Representative that does not apply equally to all U. S. Citizens. All existing laws that do not meet this criteria shall be amended or declared null and void."

A recent book by Mark Levin "The Liberty Limits" describes how our nation has breached the limits of the Constitution. He points out that our "founding fathers" with their keen vision provided two methods to control our 21st century run away Congress. Under the 10th Amendment the individual States have power outside of Congress, power to bypass Congress and call a convention to amend the U. S. Constitution. Many have concerns that the Obama Care health laws of 2012 will not apply to Congressional members the same as they do to the nation's citizens.

How can Congress expect citizens not to be extremely irate and view any and all in-equalities of the Federal Government in a similar fashion as our forefathers viewed the unjust "Kingly Rights" of the English Crown?

In retrospect, America's founders felt honored to serve their colonial constituents. They fully understood the suffering the Colonials underwent to gain their freedom and liberties. Today's congressional representatives with their exclusive elite clubs have long forgotten Rutherford's "Lex Rex" "For the people of the people by the people" We must be a nation of laws not men.

Chapter 22
James Gillespie and Printing of North Carolina Currency (Stabilization of North Carolina's Economy)

During and following the Revolutionary War, the Federal Continental dollar became less and less valuable. The new nation hoped that victory over Britain would stop the Continental's deprecation in value. Devaluation of the Continental reached one hundred Continentals to one silver dollar. The saying arose, "not worth a Continental".

The Federal Government desperately searched for a means to stabilize the country's currency and passed legislation that was hoped would help the economy. Old Continentals were retired with the issuance of new dollars. Most states enacted death penalties for counterfeiting. During the Revolution, in 1780, the Continental became worthless, approaching a value of one thousand to one dollar. Worthless payments to the Continental troops undercut troop morale and encouraged desertions for General Washington. Washington, with much sorrow, shot a number of his troops to prevent his disgruntled, unpaid, freezing and homesick troops from continuing to desert. Soldiers became very frustrated over the worthless Continental and many refused to serve and complained bitterly that the money they sent home to their families was worthless.

During these trying times of the Revolution the accelerating instability of the new nation's paper monies created a greater threat to independence than British attacks. North Carolina's provisional Government faced an empty treasury and inability to secure loans. Therefore, following the war, to alleviate the currency crisis in North Carolina and to pay honorably the heroic revolutionary soldiers, Governor Martin supported printing new paper currency to boost North Carolina's economy. A General

Assembly of 1783 was scheduled to discuss and resolve the state's huge currency crisis.

The General Assembly was held in Hillsborough, on April 18th 1783, with Alexander Martin presiding. Martin and assembly members faced an enormous economic challenge. They decided to authorize the printing of new paper currency valued at one hundred thousand pounds and to redeem over a schedule all of the paper currency in circulation. The new currency was authorized to be printed in forty, twenty-five and two shilling denominations. John Geddie and James Gillespie were appointed to supervise the printing of the new currency and number the bills. John Hunt and Benjamin McCulloch were appointed commissioners to sign and deliver the bills to the treasury.

During the new nation's economic crisis and following the war, North Carolina's enforcement of its State Constitution was often ineffective, especially, relative to the remaining issues of the Paris Peace Treaty. The State's Constitution did not provide an effective framework for dealing with the State's huge currency crisis relative to the worthlessness of its paper currency. Many complained that the General Assembly was too hasty in issuing paper money and should have placed a moratorium on lawsuits for debts. In this regard, through the sponsored legislation of James Gillespie, wives of dead war veterans were excused of all their debts. Fortunately through the leadership of dedicated Scots-Irishmen, like Governor Martin, and legislators like James Gillespie, North Carolina successfully provided an effective structure for the State's economy to recover during the new nation's economic crisis.

In retrospect, the new country under the Articles of Confederation was powerless to collect funds other than through loans or involuntary payments from the States.

(Victor Carnes, in his year 2000 thesis "Anti-Federalist Lives: The Jay Treaty, The Republican Party, and North Carolina", describes how James Gillespie was selected to a commission to print North Carolina's new currency to assist in the state's post war economic challenge. Carnes's thesis supported his degree of Master of Arts at the University of North Carolina under Don Higgenbotham, his University's adviser.)

With the State's economic crisis worsening, Governor Martin called a special assembly to approve the printing of new currency. Governor Martin selected James Gillespie to head a special commission to determine how best to print new currency for the state. Meanwhile, Caswell was elected Governor and soon requested and commissioned Gillespie to travel to Philadelphia to procure plates and paper to begin, immediately, printing North Carolina's new paper currency.

Gillespie, understanding the secrecy and urgency of his mission, made the, rugged, long trip to Philadelphia from his plantation in the Village of Grove by buggy in the freezing, snowy, winter of January 1786 to procure special printing plates and fine quality printing paper.

Benjamin Franklin, who recently returned from his peacemaking duties in France, advised James Gillespie as to the best grade of paper and design of plates for printing North Carolina's new currency. Gillespie obtained, under the strictest security measures, printing plates embossed with finely detailed leaf grains. Prior to making the printing plates, Gillespie sought the guidance and support of Benjamin Franklin's printing operation in Philadelphia. To prevent counterfeiting, Gillespie had the plates for printing North Carolina's new currency intricately designed. North Carolina used Gillespie's printing plates for many years to print the state's paper money. Gillespie's efforts greatly assisted North Carolina in resolving the state's currency problem.

Finally, Gillespie obtained North Carolina legislative authority for reimbursement of the expenses he incurred in procuring the new currency's printing plates and paper. On May 31, 1786, North Carolina finally reimbursed Gillespie for his efforts.

After ratifying the U.S. Constitution, North Carolina reluctantly agreed to abide by Constitutional provisions restricting the minting and printing of currency by individual states. The fate of North Carolina's currency, issued between 1786 and 1787, deserves remembering.

In 1810, the State Assembly chartered a state bank to retire the old Carolina currency that served many years as the main medium of exchange for the state. It appeared stabilization of the North Carolina economy, following the revolution, would have been difficult without the many North Carolina shillings printed with James Gillespie's plates and durable paper. In 1809, North Carolina's state currency changed from pounds, shillings and pence, to dollars and cents. In 1810 when the "old rugged dollar" was retired, Carolinians continued to desire the "old rugged dollar" as the standard for currency. James Gillespie's efforts through the January's wintry weather of 1786 proved very fortunate for North Carolina, considering the new currency lessened the state's dire economic crisis.

Chapter 23
James Gillespie's Congressional Service

The 6th Wilmington, North Carolina Congressional District elected James Gillespie to four terms in the U.S. Congress, i.e. the third, fourth, fifth, and eighth Congresses. James was the first U. S. Congressman from North Carolina's 6th District elected on March 4, 1793.

The Third U. S. Congress (March 1793)

The Third United States Congress met at Congressional Hall in Philadelphia during the 5th and 6th years of George Washington's Presidency, from March 1793 to March 1795. All of Philadelphia, especially members of Congress and President Washington, became very frightened over the city's yellow fever epidemic. Congress adjourned and left the city along with George and Martha Washington. Over five thousand people died of Philadelphia's dreaded fever. The risk of fever finally subsided in September and Congress returned to resume legislative business.

James Gillespie was an Anti-Federalist Congressman and greatly opposed the Jay Treaty supported by Alexander Hamilton, George Washington, John Adams, John Jay, Pinckney and other Federalists. Gillespie and other Anti-Ffederalists viewed the Jay Treaty, authored by John Jay, as a ransom payment to Britain to prevent their attack of America's merchant ships on the high seas. The Treaty easily passed the Federalist controlled Senate. The Republican controlled House of Representatives controlled by Anti-Federalists such as Macon and Gillespie, with Vice President Jefferson, opposed passage. The bill only passed the Senate by one vote. The Jay Treaty did not deter Britain's provocations for the War of 1812.

Gillespie was disappointed that his long term friend, Senator Martin parted from the Democratic Republican

Party, and voted for most of the issues supported by the Federalists. Martin lost Republican support when he supported the "Alien Rights" Act. During this period, Martin gradually lost much of his Republican support.

Martin's political opponent in the 1790's was William Davie. Davie's perfidy was well known among the Anti-Federalist camp. Martin declared "Davie, my continuing nemesis, is as ambitious as Julius Caesar. My fellow Republicans would be wise to keep a close watch on his political moves as his thirst for fame is insatiable."

Terms of the Jay Treaty specified that America was to re-pay Britain for its Revolutionary War losses and early colonial loans to America. Considering that the British burned and looted his Golden Grove Plantation, Congressman Gillespie was livid over Congressional passage of the Jay Treaty.

Jay an aristocratic New York lawyer, along with Adams, showed much partiality to Britain during America's 1783 Peace and Alliance negotiations with Britain and France. Jay, and especially Adams, constantly irritated Benjamin Franklin during the British Peace negotiations in Paris. Franklin, like Gillespie, considered that America owed much gratitude and allegiance to France for ensuring America's victory at Yorktown through a French naval blockade that blocked a water escape by Cornwallis. Not only did France provide many thousands of troops but also large sums of money. Through Franklin's keen negotiating skills, the American envoy convinced the French negotiators to lend the revolutionary cause the money it needed. His clever Paris negotiating ensured an alliance with France and a Peace Treaty with Britain, viewed by the new nation as a masterpiece.

Congressman Gillespie wrote his wife, Dorcus, many letters from Philadelphia from 1793 to 1795, stating his opinion about the Federalists. In one letter he remarked "These Federalist should show better recognition and indebtedness to France for the French ensuring America's Independence, and should support France in their war recently declared with Britain. My fellow Congressmen are continually voicing their concern over the future possibility of war with Britain."

The Gillespies and their many Scots- Irish Presbyterian friends did not forget, nor forgive, the British for burning their homes and many Presbyterian Churches across the Carolina Countryside. Jefferson was so disturbed at Washington's support of the Jay Treaty that he avoided speaking to the president.

The Republicans did not fully recognize, with the increase of Federalists wealth, that political support was beginning to swing in their favor. When the "Jay Treaty" passed Congress, the Anti-Federalists were horrified. Primary supporters of the Treaty were the merchants of New York, New Jersey, Pennsylvania and Maryland. These New England merchants through British pacification protected their huge English market which ensured their own selfish gain.

During this period, the Administration was very concerned about possible war with Britain. The Republican leaders, with a majority in the House, made light over the Federalist's prediction of war. The Anti-Federalists began a huge public outcry against the Treaty with parades, speeches, petitions and effigies. The British claimed that America's debt was three million pounds, but after much argument and review, a Treaty commission found the British Creditor claims were extremely inflated. The Commission reached a settlement for 600,000 pounds.

America passed a direct Federal excise in an effort to pay for the Treaty settlement. In 1795, the assembly set the tax at 8 pence per 100. Payment of pending Treaty terms imposed severe financial burdens on the many low-income North Carolina farmers. Their financial burden created by the Treaty threatened possible loss of their homesteads.

Fortunately, America's financial burden was relieved when Congress in 1802 canceled the Jay Treaty debts.

The Jay Treaty possibly benefited America by applying pressure on Spain to sign the Madrid Treaty that eventually settled the American-Spanish Florida Boundary dispute. The Madrid Treaty provided American navigational rights on the Mississippi River and possession of the Mississippi Territory.

In contrast, the Jay Treaty soon provided a major political benefit to the Republicans stemming from public opinion and outcry over the Treaty; especially from citizens like James Gillespie whose homes the British looted and burned. The Treaty provided a powerful stimulus for the Republican Party with Jefferson on his way to an 1800 glorious presidential victory.

The Jay Treaty was a heated topic of discussion across America. Meanwhile in Chapel Hill, North Carolina, in 1795, Congressman Gillespie's son David as President of UNC's Philanthropic debate society chose the Jay Treaty as his subject for debate. Other members of the Philanthropic society for many days debated the pros and cons of the Jay Treaty. Unanimously, the Debate Society members decided against the Treaty. David Gillespie wrote his main composition, for the 1795 school year regarding the controversial Treaty.

In 1794, Congressman Gillespie supported the construction of America's first six sailing war frigates; included were the U. S. S. Constitution and U.S.S. Pennsylvania. These sailing war ships, fitted with newer lighter weight and faster firing cannons from Scotland, were needed for protection of American merchant ships on the high seas.

Serving in Congress with Gillespie were his close North Carolina Anti-Federalist friends, Timothy Bloodworth and Benjamin Hawkins. Hawkins served in the U.S. Senate from 1789 through 1795. When Hawkins resigned from the Congress, President Washington appointed him Superintendent of Indian Affairs. Supported by his Creek common-law wife, Hawkins became principal agent for the Creeks. During the Ellicott-Gillespie Florida Survey, Hawkins was instrumental in ensuring that the Creeks allowed safe passage of David Gillespie's survey party through the dangerous Indian occupied swamps of Florida.

Hawkins' control over the Creeks apparently saved David Gillespie's life. During the survey, the Creeks attacked Gillespie and his surveying crew. They miraculously stopped short of murdering young David.

The Fourth United States Congress (March 1795)

Partisan battles raged throughout Washington's second term. Political battles flamed throughout Philadelphia between the Federalists and Anti-Federalists. Hamilton's marriage problems were used by the Anti-Federalists led by Jefferson to the fullest political advantage. Britain was at war with France with the Americans divided over the two. Hamilton and many of the Federalists supported Britain while most of the Anti-Federalists backed France.

James served in the fourth United State Congress, which met in Philadelphia from March 4, 1795 to March 31, 1797. North Carolina's Fifth Congressional district elected Gillespie and Nathaniel Macon, close Congressional Allies, to the Fourth U. S. Congress. Both Macon and Gillespie were staunch Anti-Federalists representing the Democratic Republican Party that held a fifty-five per cent House majority. In the Senate from North Carolina were two close friends of Gillespie's, Martin and Bloodworth. Alexander Martin had sided with the Federalists over the Alien and Sedition Act, and Timothy Bloodworth remained a staunch Anti-Federalist.

Representing Virginia in the Fourth United States Congress was James Madison. Madison, with Hamilton's assistance, was a driving force and key figure in drafting America's Constitution at the 1787 Constitutional Convention that both Governor Davie and Alexander Martin from North Carolina attended. They both departed without signing the draft of the Constitution.

The Fourth Congress, during Washington's last two years as president, enacted very little major legislation. The Fourth United States Congress: (1) admitted Tennessee as a state to the union, (2) seated Andrew Jackson (Old Hickory) a Scots- Irish Presbyterian to the Congress, and (3) ratified the Pinckney- Godoy Treaty (Madrid Treaty) with Spain.

David Gillespie and Ellicott successfully implemented a provision of this treaty better known as the Florida Southern Boundary Survey. Successful negotiations and fulfillment of this treaty provided America with full rights to ship the country's commercial goods down the Mississippi River along with rights to settle the Mississippi Territory.

George Washington delivered his farewell address. For Washington's grand departure, Congress selected a Congressional Committee to provide what everyone anticipated would be a glowing, grand, farewell to the "Father of the New Nation". Selected for the congressional committee were Andrew Jackson, Nathaniel Macon, James Gillespie and several other Anti-Federalists. When the committee met to vote on the Congressional bill, unexpectedly, they debated for several days before approval. Among the Congressmen who voted Nay for disapproval of Washington's glowing Congressional farewell were Jackson, Macon and Gillespie. Many Jeffersonians never forgave Washington for his express support of the Jay Treaty. Jefferson rarely spoke to Washington after he sided with Northern merchants and pushed the Jay Treaty through Congress for approval.

The Fifth United States Congress (March 1797)

The fifth United States Congress met from March 1797 through March 1799. During this session of Congress, John Adams was President and Thomas Jefferson Vice President.

For the Fifth Congress Gillespie represented the Fifth Wilmington District and served with Nathaniel Macon. Serving in the Fifth Congress in the Senate was James Gillespie's staunch Congressional ally Timothy Bloodworth. In 1798, Timothy Bloodworth found out through Benjamin Hawkins, the former North Carolina Senator and new Indian Agent to Florida, that James' eldest son, David, miraculously survived a Creek Indian attack on his Florida survey party. Bloodworth, upon getting the joyful news of Congressman Gillespie's son David's survival, rode full bore out to The Village of Grove to inform David's mother Dorcus Gillespie.

Bloodworth was a close friend of Congressman Gillespie over many years, through the American Revolution and North Carolina's Constitutional assemblies. Bloodworth lived in Wilmington and owned a farm in Burgaw ,in the countryside, a short distance from James' Duplin County plantation. Macon, Gillespie, and Bloodworth were three of the first charter members of North Carolina's "Jefferson Party". These Jeffersonians formed North Carolina's Warren Junta Club. The Warren Junta provided enormous support and was instrumental in Jefferson's election of 1800. Earlier in North Carolina's House of Commons, in 1783, Gillespie and Bloodworth opposed the State's support of the Paris, British Peace, Treaty with ludicrous terms that Loyalists were to be paid for their war losses if they hadn't bore arms against the revolutionaries.

The major legislation during the Fifth United States Congress was establishment of the Navy and Marine Corps, The terms of XYZ Affair and the Alien Sedition Acts were especially controversial. The XYZ Affair was prompted by Adam's attempt to resolve naval issues with France for confiscation of over three hundred American merchant ships. The Anti-Federalists considered the XYZ Affair as a diplomacy failure by Adams. The Anti-Federalists felt that Adams undermined positive French relations established by Benjamin Franklin.

The Federalists supported the "Alien Sedition Acts" signed by Adams. Terms of the Alien Sedition Act were viewed by the Anti- Federalists as purposely directed at American French aliens and caused very hard feelings between America and France. Alien Acts provided for deportation of aliens and issued requirements for Alien Citizenship. The Sedition Act made it a crime to publish writings against the U.S. Government.

The Marine Corps was successful in the invasion of Tripoli to defeat Barbary Coast pirates raiding American shipping. America forced Tripoli to sign a Treaty not to attack the nation's merchant ships and to cease demanding ransom for not attacking our ships as president George Washington had unbelievably paid.

Following the closing session of the Fifth Congress, in the wintry, January, weather of 1800, Gillespie fell on the icy streets of Washington and broke his hip. For several months, James was not able to return home to his North Carolina, Wilmington "Fifth District" to campaign. Thus, Gillespie lost his election to the Sixth United States Congress.

Unable to travel to North Carolina due to his broken hip, Congressman Gillespie was convalescing in Georgetown's City Tavern in Washington's freezing weather. He recuperated for several months in Georgetown, while his beloved wife Dorcus hovered near death with pneumonia at their Duplin County, Village of Grove plantation. Gillespie was unable to journey home, by stagecoach, to his Plantation to tend to family affairs, plantation business, and his Congressional re-election.

Meanwhile, William Hill, a Federalist attorney from Wilmington won enough votes in the 1800 Sixth Congressional election to narrowly defeat Congressman Gillespie.

In 1800, Bloodworth and Gillespie as staunch Jeffersonians campaigned long and hard with the support of North Carolina's Warren Junta, to ensure the election of Jefferson. They allied with Nathaniel Macon in their Presidential campaigning.

Meanwhile, in Philadelphia, Macon and Willie Jones were key leaders in the Marache Club. The Marache Club hosted the Republican Caucus that nominated Jefferson for President, and Aaron Burr for Vice President.

The 1800 presidential election used America's Electoral College rules which resulted in total chaos. Jefferson and Burr each received an equal member of electoral votes. Under the Constitution at this time the candidate who received the greatest number of electoral votes became President and the candidate with second greatest number became the Vice President.

The Democratic Republicans planned that one elector would not cast a second vote. The selected elector forgot and cast both of his votes. Therefore, Burr and Jefferson received an equal number of votes.

To settle the 1800 Presidential election, the House of Representative met in state caucuses to determine who won the most state delegations. The Federalists controlled the House, and obviously voted for Burr. Thus, Jefferson had difficulty in obtaining the required nine states for a majority. Over seven days the House cast 35 ballots. Each time Jefferson obtained only eight states; not the required nine. The Federalists of Delaware, Maryland, and Vermont finally cast blank votes, which allowed Jefferson to win the required nine state majority. The Jefferson –Burr contested election resulted in the 12th Amendment that required Vice President votes in future elections to be cast separately. Jefferson believed Burr was dishonest and politically manipulated his many Federalists friends in an attempt to steal the election. Thereafter, he never trusted Burr again.

Gillespie would have cast his congressional vote for Jefferson, but his unfortunate fall broke his hip and caused his election defeat. With a broken hip, Gillespie was unable to return to his home district to campaign and a federalist aristocrat attorney, Hill, narrowly defeated him. Gillespie's aggressive Jeffersonian allies led by Macon, Williams, Stanford, Alston, Stone and Spaight, to the greatest extent made up for Gillespie's absence from the House of Representatives. With the election of Jefferson, North Carolina was very jubilant. Duplin's Jeffersonians were ecstatic over Jefferson's victory. They celebrated for several days, throwing a magnificent party at Pearsall's Tavern in the Village of Grove. .Jefferson's election celebrations continued with a glorious party hosted by Gillespie and Bloodworth in downtown Wilmington.

In the election of 1800, the Jeffersonian Republicans gained control of the new nation's political system with their landslide win in both houses and the Presidency. These freedom loving Scots-Irishmen continued to control America's elections with the presidential victories of Madison and Monroe.

Finally, in 1824, John Quincy Adams, colluded with Henry Clay to steal the election away from Andrew Jackson, the people's choice, who won both the popular vote and had initially the largest number of electoral votes. With the election of John Quincy Adams, political control swung back for one term to the Whigs, as the successors to the Federalists. The Anti-Federalists organized as Jackson Democrats were furious over the election of Adams by the electoral vote, with the Clay switches, not the popular vote.

Jackson in his loud, outspoken, manner decried "Clay and Adams have struck a corrupt bargain" when Clay swung his electoral votes to Adams and was then appointed Secretary of State by Adams. "Old Hickory", the people's choice with his many Scots-Irish supporters for the election of 1828, was ready for the northern politicians. Jackson won the White House by a landslide. A people's election it surely proved to be. Following the swearing in ceremonial for President Jackson, the White House was totally over-run by the common every-day people with their jubilant celebrations. Jackson's occupancy of the White House was delayed for several weeks to repair major damage caused by the jubilations of the overjoyed mob.

The Eighth United States Congress (1803-1805)

James Gillespie was re-elected to the eighth Congress which met from March 1803 through March 1805. Under Jefferson's first term as President, the Anti-Federalists greatly expanded America's boundaries, with the purchase of the Louisiana Territory from France.

In 1804, the Navy, using the newly launched Constitution sailing war ship, burned America's pirate held Philadelphia war ship to prevent the vessel's continued use by the pirates. America's bold naval action ended the Barbary Pirate attacks on America's merchant ships.

In 1804, Aaron Burr held a pistol dual with Alexander Hamilton and Hamilton was mortally wounded. In 1804, impeachment trials began against Burr for treason relative to his taking Spanish bribes, along with General Wilkinson, for supporting Spain in the Spaniards attempts to control the Mississippi Territories. General Wilkinson and Burr over the 1790's, as discovered by David Gillespie and Ellicott during their Madrid Treaty Survey, were entangled in a Spanish treason plot concerning payments of gold. Ellicott reported these plots of treason to Secretary of State Pickering. Under Adam's Federalist Administration, Congress did little to investigate Burr and Wilkinson on charges of treason. Until near the end of Jefferson's first presidential term, the Federal Government ignored Burr and Wilkinson's scheme for a Spanish territory on American land.

Part VII- Presbyterian Support of Higher Education in America

The Scots-Irish Presbyterian emigrants brought to America their ancestors' appreciation for education. Presbyterian educational philosophy was engrained many years earlier during their first reformation. Their philosophy centered on Knox's "Book of Discipline" and was influenced by Calvin's principles. The Presbyterian reformation demanded that Scotland's citizens develop a high level of education to ensure they were well versed in scripture. As evidenced during Scotland's 18th century enlightenment, Presbyterian educational philosophies were highly rewarding. Scotland was the envy of the world for their unbelievable technological achievements.

Experience through the centuries taught these Scots-Irish Presbyterians and they well understood: "The Liberated human mind seeks education as the eagle aspires to soar skyward when set free". Fortunately, Presbyterians extensively increased the knowledge of colonial Americans. They greatly advanced human understanding by founding America's first four Universities. These seminaries, which focused on the political and religious philosophy of the renowned Scottish Philosophers, played a crucial role in educating many founding fathers. America's first four Universities, initially seminaries, were Harvard, the College of William and Mary, Yale, and Princeton. The majority of America's founding fathers were educated in these four institutions of higher education.

In North Carolina, the many Presbyterians and Presbyterian ministers, including Caldwell and McCorkle were graduates of the College of New Jersey, which later became Princeton University. Supported by legislation written into North Carolina's Constitution, the devoted Presbyterian graduates of Princeton helped open the doors of the nation's first public University to enroll students, the

University of North Carolina. Around America's countryside, the renowned ministers Cotton Mather and Witherspoon and the many ministers in Carolina such as Caldwell and McCorkle greatly influenced America's higher educational system and instilled the political and religious philosophies that drove the Presbyterian Reformation. These ministers fully understood the enormous importance of education in founding an educated and free nation.

Chapter 24
Presbyterian Minister's Huge Contribution to the Founding of Colonial America's Universities (Presbyterian Educational Influence in Colonial North Carolina.)

By the mid 1700's, two hundred thousand Scots-Irish had emigrated to America. Many of these immigrants who first settled in Pennsylvania and Virginia migrated down the Appalachian Trail into Mecklenburg, Rowan, and Alamance Counties of North Carolina. Many settled in their customary clannish villages.

Raised within families of strong Presbyterian doctrine, these Scots-Irish were emphatic supporters of civil liberties and staunch supporters of education. These villagers insisted in their ministers proclaiming the gospel of salvation. Coupled with their religious salvation, with rare exception, they opened their small classical schools. Minister Foote's "Sketches of North Carolina" portrays the significant role the Presbyterian ministers played in supporting higher education in the Tar Heel state. Among the small classical schools were Sugar Creek, Poplar Tent, Bethany, Thyatira, and Rocky River, all within Rowan and Mecklenburg counties.

When the colonial Governor supported a school in Edenton, he allowed only a schoolmaster from the Church of England. The Scots-Irish petitioned the Governor for a chartered college in Mecklenburg with a Presbyterian schoolmaster. Initially the Crown granted a charter for Presbyterians to found their Queens College. Soon, the Governor repealed the charter in fear that the school would become a Presbyterian meeting place for seeking liberty from the Crown.

These determined and educational enthusiastic, Presbyterians continued their small college without a charter. King George's fears of the Presbyterian's meetinghouse proved especially true with the drafting of their Mecklenburg Declaration of Independence in the halls of Queens College.

The Revolutionary War closed Queen's College with British troops using the school as a hospital. The British troops encamped at Reverend Caldwell's home and burned most of his ministry records. Caldwell, due to his inflammatory preaching against the British, enraged Cornwallis. The British offered a large ransom for Minister Caldwell's head.

Following the revolution, the North Carolina legislation, sponsored by Alexander Martin, chartered a college on the old Queen's campus with the charter name "Liberty Hall". The trustees included Samuel McCorkle, Thomas Polk, Abraham Alexander, David Caldwell and Waightstill Avery.

In 1785, Duplin's Scots-Irish clan led by General James Kenan and U. S. Congressman and State Senator James Gillespie, chartered the Grove Academy in the Village of Grove. These colonial Patriots fully understood that without education it is virtually impossible to ensure an educated electorate to preserve freedom.

James Gillespie instilled in his two sons, David and Joseph, the critical importance of obtaining a sound education. James constantly reminded his two sons of their Gillespie ancestor's educational philosophy taught by the great scholars of Scotland .i. e. "The liberated human mind aspires education as the eagle aspires to soar skyward when set free."

James' sons, David and Joseph, prior to their enrolling in the 1795 and 1796 classes at the University of North Carolina (America's first public university to enroll students), attended the Grove Academy preparatory school. Over the years, Duplin's small local village academy, the Grove Academy graduated such impressive alumni as Vice President William Rufus DeVane King of Sampson

County. King was also graduated from the University of North Carolina in 1803. He like David Gillespie was a member of the Philanthropic Debate Society. Like the students of McCorkle, Congressman Gillespie's sons, David and Joseph, were schooled and well prepared for North Carolina's first public university. In his early teen years, David received schooling in mathematics from the Grove Academy, and training in astronomy and surveying from his father.

Presbyterian educational influence across colonial America

Another example of early Presbyterian Scots-Irish influence on higher education was that of John Witherspoon the sixth President of Princeton "University. Witherspoon was a signer of the Declaration of Independence for New Jersey.

Witherspoon was a graduate of Edinburgh University. He received his doctorate degree from Saint Andrews from which Congressman James Gillespie's' Scottish, 17th century, ancestors George and Patrick Gillespie were also graduates before becoming renowned theologians.

The Witherspoon families over the years in Scotland, like the Gillespie's, were Presbyterian ministers and leading Covenanters. Witherspoon was the leader of the Popular Party for the Church of Scotland. The College of New Jersey (today's Princeton University) Board of Trustees, in 1754, persuaded Witherspoon to leave Scotland to become administrator of Princeton. At this time, he brought his family to New Jersey to join him in Princeton. He found the College in poor financial shape. He immediately began to improve the college finances with an aggressive speaking campaign to the College of William and Mary in Williamsburg, Virginia.

Early pioneers of colonial American education included the Mathers of Boston. Cotton and his father

Increase were among the many Presbyterian ministers from Scotland and Ireland who settled in New England. Increase Mather was the sixth president of Harvard University.

During Mather's Harvard tenure a feud broke out among the University's religious leaders. In frustration, Mather left Harvard and gave his support to a small Presbyterian seminary school named Collegiate. The state of Connecticut supported the founding of Collegiate College. The Mathers and several other trustees of the small seminary solicited Elihu Yale president of the British East India Company to pledge a large grant to Collegiate. To honor Yale's most generous gift, the seminary's trustees re-named the Collegiate school Yale.

Mather also influenced colonial America through his many publications. His publication "Essay to Do Good" prompted Benjamin Franklin to pioneer the founding of a hospital and volunteer fire departments in Philadelphia.

Chapter 25
The University of North Carolina (UNC): The New Nation's First Public University (Reference Kemp Battles - "The History of the University of North Carolina")

State Constitutional Language for Founding America's First Public University UNC

When England disapproved their charter to begin Queen's College, the Scots-Irish of Mecklenburg became outraged. Mecklenburg's University delegate Waightsville Avery ,along with James Gillespie and other Scots-Irish delegates, demanded that the 1776 North Carolina General Assembly provide Constitutional language for a state public university. The language in North Carolina's Constitution; therefore, reads, "A school or schools shall be established by the legislature for the convenient education of youth, with such salaries to the masters, paid by the public, as may enable them to instruct at low prices and all useful learning shall be duly encouraged in one or more Universities."

James Gillespie, for a period of time with his high acumen, provided administrative service to his colleague and personal friend Governor Alexander Martin. Gillespie and Governor Martin, provided much support for North Carolina's first public University. Governor Martin served as the first President of the University's Board of Trustees. Martin served as board trustee president until his death in 1807.

As a State Senator and U.S. Congressman, James Gillespie continued his support for U.N.C. at Chapel Hill. He fully demonstrated his support by sending his sons David and Joseph to the first entering class of 1795 and the class of 1796, respectively. Other Duplin supporters of

U.N.C. were the Dickson's, close family friends of the Gillespies. Robert Dickson was on the University's Board of Trustees and William, his brother, sent his son Lewis to the class of 1796.

1789 General Assembly Charter for U.N.C.

North Carolina's 1789 General Assembly, Constitutional Ratification Convention, met on Gillespie Street, Fayetteville, N.C. in 1789 and approved a charter for the University of North Carolina. Supporters included Benjamin Hawkins, Alexander Martin, James Gillespie, Robert Dickson, Nathaniel Macon and William Davie. Davie was such a driving force for the University that his contemporaries referred to Davie as the "Father of the University". In 1776, many of the Assembly delegates who met in Halifax, including James Gillespie of Duplin and Colonel John Gillespie of Guilford County, ensured North Carolina's Constitution contained language to support a public University. The Assembly Charter language read "In all well regulated governments it is the indefensible duty of every legislature to consult the happiness of a using generation and endeavor to fit them for an honorable discharge of the social duties of life by discharge of the aid duties of life by paying the strictest attention to their education and that a university supported by permanent funds and well-endowed would have the most direct tendency to answer the above purpose."

University's Doors Opened and Welcomed the New Students for the First Class of 1795

Following construction of the University's first dorm classroom known today as "Old East" in 1793-1794, the new University struggled to find Professors who would accept the meager salaries offered. After hiring Professor Kerr, in February 1795, and McCorkle earlier in December, the Board of Trustees, despite the cold frigid February weather, opened North Carolina and America's first public university.

Citizens of the State of N. C. were thrilled over the opening of their new University, especially the people of the Scots-Irish Village of Grove. David Gillespie, son of Congressman Gillespie, excitedly packed for several weeks in anticipation of his journey to Chapel Hill.

Congressman Gillespie, recently returned from Congress in Philadelphia, fighting against the Jay Treaty's passage, expressed to Robert Dickson, Alexander Martin and several other Board Directors the importance of the new University's providing his son David and other students with the latest books in math and the sciences, and especially books in astronomy and surveying. James and his close friend, William Dickson, Duplin's clerk of the court, discussed various means of procuring textbooks needed for the students.

They explored the possibility of ordering the latest books from Belfast, Ulster. Luckily, the Gillespies and Dicksons found a few books for David's schooling. They borrowed several books from the Grove Academy preparatory school. Among the books recommended for the new University, were Samuel Rutherford's "Lex Rex", Mather's "Essay to Do Good", Bunyan's "Pilgrim Progress" and several of Congressman James Gillespie's books of astronomy and surveying..

On a cold February evening of 1795, prior to young David Gillespie's departure for Chapel Hill, friends of David and the Gillespie family gathered at the Pearsall Tavern for an exciting evening to celebrate David's enrollment in the State's new public University at Chapel Hill. Among the invited guests were the Routledges, Pearsalls, Dicksons, Stallings, their teen age daughters and sons and David's Grove Academy classmates.

Early the next morning, Joseph, David's younger brother, and Louis Dickson eagerly loaded the Gillespie family coach with David's large leather trunk. After kissing his mother, Dorcus, and hugging his father and the Dickson family, David said goodbye to his family and friends.

Both Louis and Joseph had plans to enter UNC after completing another year of preparatory study at the Grove Academy. After ensuring all luggage, horse feed and food were loaded for the journey, the young lads eagerly climbed onboard the Gillespie coach. They drove into the Grove Village to the famous Pearsall spring to fill their canteens and a large water barrel with the cool spring mineral water to ensure that they, as well as their two bay horses, had sufficient drinking water for their two-day trip to Chapel Hill.

After bidding farewell to their many friends gathered around the Village of Grove's old spring, the three young lads climbed aboard the Gillespie's two horse coach and headed out from the small Scots-Irish Village onward through Hillsboro. They arrived in Chapel Hill late the next evening.

Upon arrival of the Duplin lads at UNC, several students, including Hinton James and several of McCorkel's former Salisbury students, welcomed Congressman Gillespie's coach as it rolled onto the University's new campus. James had arrived earlier from Wilmington, on February 15th, and anxiously awaited the arrival of other students and professors. Joyfully, he greeted David. David exclaimed to Hinton, "Why didn't you stop at the Grove on your way up the Great Duplin road from Burgaw? You were welcome to have made the journey with us." Hinton replied, smiling, "I would have welcomed the ride considering my week long trek through the frigid wintry rain and snow".

For the next several months, the students were busy adapting to their new campus life under the supervision, and tutorage of the University's first two Professors, McCorkle and Kerr.

During the spring of 1795, David noticed the literary (acrostic poetry) works of George Norton, a roving poet, who visited the new campus. David Gillespie after reading several of Norton's poems recognized his talent and became interested in buying a poem for his younger sister, Jane, who was eleven years of age at this time. David purchased the following acrostic for his sister Jane:

"In twilight morning's sweet and pleasing beam,
Upon my mind breaks like a morning dream,
Constraining smiles to intermix with tears,
Yet holding fast the scenes of former years,
Gone with the light and shade of joys and fears,
We soon shall close the bright and pleasant scene,
Rejoice with smiles or languish into spleen,
I hail the dawn my constant friends to see,
Glad to rejoice with those who feel for me,
Hope wing me smiling from my long retreat,
The crop was bitter but the crown is sweet."

Selection of Board of Trustees and First Professors

Following the charter, Davie was a dynamo in financing the university. On November 10, 1790, the New University's Board of Trustees, held their second meeting in Fayetteville on Gillespie Street and elected Alexander Martin as their Chairman for their Board of Trustees. The Board, also, selected McCorkle, the son of a Waxhaw's Scots-Irish Presbyterian Minister, to the Board's trustees. In December of 1794, the Board of Trustees selected McCorkle as U.N.C.'s "First Professor". In 1795, the Board did not have sufficient funds for a President of the University so McCorkle's duties included both President and First Professor. McCorkle, to ensure peace and harmony with the Board of Trustees, declined the First Professor position.

The professors for the new university were McCorkle-Professor of Moral and Political Philosophy and History, Kerr- Professor of Languages, Richards- Professor of French and English, Harris- Professor of Mathematics, and Delvaux and Holmes tutors in the Grammar School.

In 1797, following the departure of Professor Harris, the University Board selected James Smiley Gillespie, a graduate of Princeton and Presbyterian minister from Guilford County as the Professor of Natural Philosophy. Natural Philosophy was similar to today's Physics. In 1798, the University's Board selected James Smiley Gillespie as their Presiding Professor. In 1799, he served as Principal of the University. The following school year James Smiley Gillespie resigned with the entire faculty, including McCorkle, due to a bitter Federalists versus Anti-Federalist feud on and around campus . (Reference Kemp Battle's, "History of the University of North Carolina)

Upon resigning from the University, Professor Gillespie moved to Kentucky, near Boonsboro, where he settled on Transylvania granted land. Gillespie opened a log cabin church-school where he served as the minister and teacher for a wilderness village. Professor Gillespie inherited several thousand acres in Franklin County, Tennessee from his father, Colonel Daniel Gillespie. For his heroic Revolutionary war service, North Carolina awarded Colonel Daniel Gillespie large land grants in Tennessee's Cumberland Valley. Professor Gillespie, until his death in 1811, lived in the Cumberland Valley, on his father, Daniel Gillespie's, land grant. Colonel Daniel Gillespie and his brother John are credited with founding the City of Greensboro, North Carolina.

Professor Gillespie, the son of Colonel Daniel Gillespie and nephew of N.C. State Senator John Gillespie, was married to Frances "Fannie" Henderson the first white child born in Kentucky. In 1775, Fannie's mother and Daniel Boone's daughter, Jemima, were rescued near Boonesboro from Shawnee Indians by Daniel Boone and Fannie's father, Samuel Henderson.

This rescue, today, is glorified in a legendary painting by Charles Wemar.

"Rescue of Fannie Henderson and Jemima Boone"

In 1775, America's 14th Colony of Transylvania elected Samuel Henderson along with Daniel Boone to their House of Delegates. The Gillespie brothers, John and Daniel, were heroes of the battle of Guilford Courthouse where they served courageously under General Nathaniel Greene.

Professor James Smiley Gillespie and David Gillespie, the first President of U.N.C's Philanthropic Society, were ancestors of Patrick and George Gillespie, the famous Presbyterian Scottish Covenanters of the 1600's. The Gillespies, like the majority of U.N.C.'s early leaders and founders, were staunch Presbyterians.

Daniel and John Gillespie's and Congressman James Gillespie's great uncle was George Gillespie, the Presbyterian minister in the early 1700's at Christiana Church. Minister Gillespie was the grandson of Scotland's renowned theologian, George Gillespie, the leader of the Westminster Assembly of the 1640's. Minister Gillespie served as a Presbyterian minister in Delaware for many years, and was the great- grandfather of Jane Knox the mother of President James Knox Polk. Jane Knox's great-great grandfather was Scotland's famous theologian John Knox. President Polk, obviously in keeping with the Gillespie and Knox family religion, was a staunch Presbyterian. Polk belonged to the Dialectic Fraternity during his college years at the University of North Carolina.

UNC Jay Treaty Disputes of the Federalists and Anti-Federalists

All of America, like U.N.C.'s professors, was deeply divided over the Jay Treaty. All of the Professors (Harris, McCorkle, and Kerr) were Presbyterians except Holmes who was a Baptist. Holmes called the Presbyterian faculty hypocrites as to their theory of virtue.

Shortly after the University opened the infidel movement in France against the Bible and religion reached America. This anti-religious movement greatly alarmed the University's Presbyterian ministers, especially ancestors of Scotland's Covenanters. Holmes the assistant professor was an advocate of Thomas Paine's "Age of Reason". Paine's book was the only book Holmes gave to the University Library. Paine's "Age of Reason" also influenced Professor Kerr, a former Presbyterian Minister.

In 1798, seven students received their diplomas from the University of North Carolina. They were the first class to be graduated from North Carolina's new public university. These seven students were graduated under the guidance of Professor James Smiley Gillespie. Professor

Gillespie was a cousin to McCorkle's wife Margaret Gillespie Steele. In the University's first graduating class of 1798 there were only seven graduates due in part to a number of students withdrawing from the University over the bitter disputes of the Jay Treaty. Six of the graduates were former students of McCorkle from his classical Salisbury School. The only other graduate was Hinton James, David Gillespie's close friend from Burgaw, near Wilmington. James was the first student to arrive when the University opened its doors. He walked through a wintry, snow, storm to reach the new campus.

The Federalists and Anti-Federalists political differences created immense discord. Due to Davie's staunch, unpleasant, Federalist political position the University experienced much unrest.

In 1796, the Gillespies and Dicksons withdrew their sons, Joseph and Lewis, from the new University as well as their financial support. In deference to the campus unrest, McCorkle chose to send his son, Alexander (Sandy), to the University of Pennsylvania.

General John Steele of Salisbury served as the U.S. Comptroller for three Presidents and was a prominent Revolutionary War hero and brother of McCorkle's wife Margaret Gillespie Steele. He wrote a scathing letter to Davie stating: "I General Steele am happy to be relieved of the humiliation of my nephew (McCorkle's son Sandy) attending an institution whose outset was characteristic by acts of ingratitude and insult toward his father Professor McCorkle."

McCorkle's wife, Margaret Gillespie Steele, was the daughter of Elizabeth Maxwell Gillespie Steele, stepdaughter of General John Steele, a war hero from Salisbury. Elizabeth Steele's first marriage was apparently to a relative of John and Daniel Gillespie, Battle of Guilford Courthouse heroes, making her a cousin to Professor James Smiley Gillespie. The McCorkles and

Steeles were close knit families and supported the selection of James Smiley Gillespie as First Professor of UNC.

During the 1799-1805 troublesome years at the University, Davie was extremely busy with his personal legislative affairs as Governor and his campaign for United States Congress. He was an ambassador to France to negotiate peace. In 1799, the Anti-Federalists and Federalists political rivalry in North Carolina and on campus at the University became extremely heated. The Anti-Federalists and Federalists students fought on and around campus. The Federalists accused Jefferson and his party's leaders of mob rule, and labeled their support of basic human rights as French-Red Republican.

The University, during the administration of President John Adams, became greatly influenced by the Philosophy of the Federalists who dominated the University. James Gillespie and his Anti-Federalists friends opposed the Davie Federalists faction imposing their overpowering Federalist's views on the University's Board of Trustees.

When the Jeffersonian Administration gained power, the Anti-Federalists were determined to neutralize the Federalists' domineering influence on the University Board. The financial step the Jeffersonians chose was very alarming for the new University. The Jefferson administration repealed the 1789- 1794 escheats intended to provide funds under the Tory confiscated land statutes.

Through leadership and his Presbyterian influence, Caldwell was able to win a compromise with the Jeffersonians. The Federalist's members of the Board of Trustees agreed to appoint a more neutral, less Federalists domineering members. They agreed to appoint more Anti-Federalists when future board openings occurred. With the election of a more diversified Board of Trustees, the Jefferson administration restored the University's rights to escheated property, and in turn Professor Caldwell received critical funding for the University.

In 1805, Governor Davie lost his bid for Congress through Anti-Federalist opposition. Feeling threatened at the university as well as humiliated and discouraged by his Congressional loss, Davie retired to Lancaster, South Carolina on a farm inherited from his uncle.

After two hundred years, the final irony is that the University's disputes and unrest became more strident than imagined by Gillespie, Dickson, McCorkle, Jones, Harris, Caldwell and other Anti-Federalists. The University had survived by accepting principles that Governor Davie as a Federalist despised. Today people view the University of North Carolina as the University of the People, for the People, by the People. Davie became an aristocrat, through wealth he married into and with political alliances. Davie did not understand the common man. Many alleged that Davie wanted the University of North Carolina to abandon the common man for the affluent.

Today, the University of North Carolina furthers many of the Gillespie-McCorkle Democratic principles of Thomas Jefferson. But it also seeks to create an enlightened elite as Davie had advocated.

Shortly after David Gillespie left the University as President of the Philanthropic Society to serve as secretary-surveyor to America's Madrid Treaty delegation, Professor Harris departed to practice law. Prior to his leaving, Harris convinced his Princeton classmate and friend Joseph Caldwell to succeed him as Professor of Mathematics. Caldwell was hired by the Board of Trustees as Harris's replacement.

Following graduation of the University's first class of 1798, James Smiley Gillespie resigned due to the turmoil of the Federalists and Anti-Federalists campus conflicts. James Smiley Gillespie served as the First Professor at U.N.C. for two long years. Fortunately an energetic and talented teacher like Joseph Caldwell agreed to take over as

First Professor following Professor Gillespie's resignation.

Caldwell led U.N.C. through hard political and financial times. Caldwell personally contributed to the University with the building of the University's observatory in 1830. The Caldwells like the Gillespies, and so many other Scots-Irish Presbyterians, from Ulster were instrumental in ensuring higher education success across America. Caldwell like many early supporters of U.N.C. attended Princeton and studied under Witherspoon. University trustees educated by Witherspoon include Martin, Davie, and McCorkle. The Professors, who were former students of Witherspoon, planned the New University's courses of instruction to be similar to those of Princeton.

University of North Carolina's First Debate Societies

In April, 1795 Professor Harris, finally, arrived from Princeton to teach Mathematics. Professor Harris introduced the students to Princeton's debate societies. Harris a former member of Princeton's Whig Debate Society had experienced the many educational and social benefits of such discourse. On June 3, 1795, Professor Harris organized the University's first debate society.

The Debate Society, to some extent, used the guidelines from Franklin's Junta (Apron Club) and practiced the Socratic approach (using gentle queries for redirection). The Society's primary objectives were: improvement in debating skills, proper English Composition, and enforcement of parliamentary rules and procedures. The latter furthered the meetings to provide moral principles, social values, and lasting friendships.

After three meetings, the Debate Society, at the suggestion of David Gillespie, was divided into the Concord and the Philanthropic sections. The Philanthropic Society at their first meeting, in August 1795, elected

Gillespie as its President.

David's father, James, and his many Presbyterian friends and associates, supported David's decision to divide the Debate Society. The Presbyterian faction of the University, led by McCorkle, supported Jeffersonian Democracy. They desired that "**LIBERTY**" be an integral part of the new debate society's motto. In addition, the Gillespies and other Presbyterians whose ancestors were Scotland's Covenanters greatly encouraged that "blue" be the primary color emblem of the University. Scotland and England referred to the Covenanters as the "blue" Whigs of Scotland. The primary color in Scotland's flag is blue. The Covenanters used blue as their primary color in their many years of fighting the Crown for religious freedom. Thus, "Carolina blue" has signified the University of North Carolina for over two centuries.

David Gillespie, remembering his ancestors long and cruel suffering and quest for liberty and freedom, happily insisted, with his father's gleeful support, in **LIBERTY** (Libertis) becoming the "Phi motto". In 1796, the Concord became known as the Dialectic Society.

The Society's President oversaw the very strict procedural rules controlled by a Censor morum, two correctors, a clerk, and a treasurer. The Censor morum inspected the conduct and morals of the members and reported before the Society as to a members conduct. The President and censor morum closely monitored the students to ensure they remained studious with good conduct so as not to impose disgrace on fellow members.

The Society, divided into three sections, held their Society meetings on Thursday evenings. The members varied their time between reading, speaking, and composing. The Society selected two readers to suggest a subject of interest for debate at their next meeting. From the readers suggested topics the Society approved a topic for reading and debate.

Initially, the most important business for the Society was the provision of books. McCorkle and his former students brought a number of books to the University, including theological readings. McCorkle, in his Moral Philosophy class, extensively read Euclid's Elements of Mathematics and Witherspoon's syllabus of lectures for Moral Philosophy. One of the first orders of business for the two debate societies was the purchase of sufficient books. Today, some of these books are enshrined in the Wilson Library Archives at the University of North Carolina.

Soon after the University chartered the Phi Society, David ,in September 21, 1795, nominated his friend Hinton James for membership and all members of the Society unanimously approved Hinton James to be a member. In October 20, 1795, David Gillespie nominated Hinton James to be President of the Society. Again all members voted for James to be their President.

On December 6, 1795, prior to adjourning for Christmas, the Phi Society again selected Gillespie to be its President. David Gillespie, serving as the Society's First President, led a number of debates, spoke on a number of subjects, and read a number of classical scientific documents to the society.

The Society extracted their readings, speeches and debates from history, books of poetry, and the London Daily, the Spectator. Many of their selected subjects were used by Franklin's Junta, and Cotton Mather's writings, and other classical and scientific writings of the day. A popular debate source was Addison and Steele's Spectator which encouraged educational points of view on major issues of the day. Like the Spectator, many of the Phi's discussions strived to enliven morality with wit, and temper it with morality. Obviously, a heated topic for discussion was the Jay Treaty.

The readings and speeches were usually serious, but

occasionally comical such as David Gillespie's "The Stuttering Soldier", and "Thoughts that arose in the mind of a Sleeping Man". David's other speeches, often selected from the recently published Murray's Grammar, also stimulated listeners.

The Trustees, between August 12 and December 15 1795, presented citations to students that excelled in composition. David Gillespie and Hinton James received several such honors. David received honors for his compositions about the "Jay Treaty" and the "Pitch and Management of the Voice". Hinton James' honored compositions included "The Commerce of Britain", "The Slave Trade" and the "History of Jupiter".

In August of 1796, America selected David Gillespie as secretary for Ellicott's survey of the Florida border with Spain. Following David's selection for this important mission, Mr. Heinz, the Philanthropic Society's new President, moved that David Gillespie should be furnished a diploma. Professors and the student body unanimously approved the proposal, and Mr. Heinz serving as President for the debate society, appointed George Levy and Edwin Ashborn to draw up the "Certificate of Scholarship" to be signed by Governor Samuel Ashe.

David Gillespie's U.N.C.'s First Diploma signed by Governor Ashe – (The original diploma signed by Governor Ashe is filed at the Library of Congress.)

****

DAVID GILLESPIE'S CERTIFICATE OF SCHOLARSHIP

September 21, 1796 (STATE SEAL-------)
State of North Carolina State Seal affixed by Governor
Sam Ashe – Governor,
Captain, General, and Commander in Chief in and over
the same State

I do hereby certify that David Gillespie is a native and citizen of this State. Son of Honorable James Gillespie one of the delegates from the State in the Congress of the U. S., is of fair and unblemished character and lately was a student in our State's first public university as appears by the testimonial under the hands of three, Charles W. Harris, professor of mathematics and natural philosophy, Samuel Holmes professor of the Latin, and William B. Richards, Professor of the French and English languages, whom I do hereby certify to be professors in said University.

In testimony where of I have herewith set my hand and caused the Great Seal of the State to herewith affixed at Asheton the 21st day of September A.D. 1796.

Signed: Honorable Governor- **Samuel Ashe**

****

Professor's signatures attached:

"We the undersigned Professors in the University of North Carolina have had under our particular care Mr. David Gillespie of this State. He has studied Greek and Latin and elementary mathematics with their application to surveying and navigation etc.

He has studied under our care Natural philosophy and astronomy. His behavior while at this place has in all respects met with our warmest appreciation.

Mr. Gillespie being about to leave the University to attend Mr. Ellicott in determining the southern boundary of the United States we have thought proper to give him this certificate." Charles W Harris-Prof. of Math and Natural Philosophy –Samuel Holmes –Prof. of Languages—W. L. Richards Prof. of French and English

Professor Harris, the son of a Scots-Irish Presbyterian minister, was instrumental in the start of the University's debate society and greatly assisted in the selection of the academia modeled after Princeton's. During his tenure, Professor Harris provided much leadership for the early administration of the University as well as scientific tutorage to advanced students such as David Gillespie and Hinton James. Unfortunately for the University, Harris departed to take over Chief Justice Ellsworth's law practice in Halifax. Harris died at a young age in 1804.

A few months prior to Professor Harris's resignation from UNC, David Gillespie, in the last week of August 1796, bade farewell to all his UNC friends and classmates to join Andrew Ellicott to help resolve the Mississippi territorial disputes with the Spaniards. David's mission involved surveying across hundreds of miles of Florida's unknown wilderness, occupied by many dangerous Indian tribes to secure a binding treaty with Spain.

Part VIII- Settlement of Territorial Disputes with Spain
Chapter 26
Florida Boundary Survey
(Ellicott, America's Commissioner of Pinckney-Goday Treaty, David Gillespie- Surveyor and Secretary)

In the 1780's, Andrew Ellicott's accurate boundary surveys settled a number of major territorial disputes among several states. His survey of the Canadian border resolved a large boundary dispute between New York and Canada. Following his territorial boundary surveys, Ellicott, in early 1790, completed his celebrated survey for George Washington of the nation's Capital. George Washington was grateful for Ellicott's excellent layout of the future capital, Washington D.C.

Washington selected Ellicott, on May 4, 1796, as Commissioner to settle the nation's critical and complicated territorial issues of the Pinckney-Goday Treaty. The Jay Treaty, between the U. S. and Britain, added pressure on Spain to agree to terms of the Pinckney-Goday Treaty. Treaty terms were designed to resolve trade and settlement problems in the Mississippi Territory.

Under the treaty, Spain provided the United States free navigation of the mighty Mississippi and the right to use New Orleans as a shipping port. Shipping via the Mississippi was vitally important to the new nation's merchants and farmers; especially the many Scots-Irish who settled on the rich farm and lowland valleys of Ohio, Kentucky and Tennessee.

For American merchants to sell their produce at Natchez or New Orleans, or ship their goods to the Gulf via the Mississippi, they had to pay tolls to the Spaniards who controlled the Mississippi and all territorial land south of the 31st parallel. To encourage Americans to abandon United States Citizenship Spain offered land grants along the Mississippi Basin. As an additional inducement, Spain offered to let Americans settle in Louisiana for free shipping rights on the Mississippi. For the inhabitants of the adjoining states of Tennessee, Kentucky, and Ohio whose farmers sorely needed a free passage for their goods, the Spaniard's inducements were quite attractive.

In preparation for his survey into the Florida wilderness, Andrew Ellicott, in late summer 1796, met in Philadelphia with various members of the U. S. Congress and Secretary of State, Timothy Pickering, to discuss his survey's difficult political problems and physical dangers that he had to face. Pickering warned of the dangers, including man eating reptiles in the Florida wilderness, and the difficult resolution of problems with the Spaniards. Ellicott needed superb diplomatic skills to maintain peace and harmony with the many Indian tribes as well as the Spaniards.

Ellicott met with various members of Congress; including Benjamin Hawkins. He considered his meeting with Hawkins especially critical since Hawkins was in high esteem and respect with the territory's many Indian tribes, especially the Creeks. The ongoing unrest of the Indians in the region greatly concerned Ellicott. Hawkins provided much advice on how to best interface with the indigenous Indian tribes on route. Hawkins assured Ellicott that he personally, as newly appointed Superintendent of Indian Affairs, would inform the many tribes of the region of America's mission and impress that America's intention was not to take over the Indian's tribal land. Senator Hawkins resigned his N. C. senate seat, and later that year he moved to southern Georgia, and thereafter chose a Creek squaw as his wife.

During Ellicott's meetings with Benjamin Hawkins, and other members of Congress, he met North Carolina's Congressman James Gillespie. Gillespie mentioned his son David's interest in serving as secretary to record the various meetings with the Spanish officials, and complete the challenging survey records.

Over a rum or two at Philadelphia's City Tavern, a favorite pub for members of Congress, Congressman Gillespie entertained Secretary of State Pickering and Ellicott with the idea of his son David's selection for the Commission. Pickering was very much impressed with David Gillespie's credentials in surveying, mathematics, and his outstanding scholastic achievements at North Carolina's new University. Pickering with the encouragement of several members of Congress unanimously selected David to serve as Ellicott's Secretary for the Madrid Treaty Survey.

David Gillespie sacrificed his college education and relinquished his leadership role in UNC'S 1795 first class to provide service to the nation's important Florida survey. David bade farewell to his friend Hinton James and all his many classmates and friends at UNC. He set off on his dangerous journey across the Florida wilderness to help resolve the new nation's critical Mississippi Territorial political and boundary issues with the Spaniards.

David's mother, Dorcus, dreaded to see her eldest son, David, leave on such a dangerous mission. She at the time was in poor health. David's father, Congressman Gillespie, and Senator Hawkins helped ease some of Mrs. Gillespie's worries by assuring her that David would be safe. Senator Hawkins assured, "I promise you the Creeks will be fully informed of who David is and that he is a personal friend of mine. David will receive much protection and support from the commission's military escort."

Joseph, David's younger brother, comforted his mother reassuring her he was man enough to protect her and his five sisters including six year old Mildred. Joseph assured his father and brother, David, he was capable of handling the numerous problems and chores on the

Gillespie plantation. He promised David that he would faithfully manage the plantation while David served America far away in the Florida wilderness. David's absence from their plantation would be even more difficult for the family since their father Congressman Gillespie would be serving in Philadelphia as North Carolina's fifth district congressional representative.

Ellicott departed from Philadelphia, September 1796, with his survey party that included young David Gillespie as secretary, Thomas Freeman as appointed surveyor, and Ellicott's 19-year-old son Andy. The survey crew passed through Pittsburgh to pick up boats, supplies and a military escort at Fort Pitt. Young Gillespie and other members of Ellicott's survey expedition left Pittsburgh in October 1796, traveling down the Ohio to the Mississippi. The expedition experienced an extremely cold winter on the Ohio River with the crew nearly freezing to death as they with much difficulty lifted boats, equipment and supplies many times around large rocks and many river ice blockages. When the exhausted, nearly starved, men reached the Ohio River's confluence with the Mississippi River, they found the junction of the rivers totally blocked with ice. Again, the crew overcame difficulty dragging their boats and supplies around the iced blockage into the Mississippi River.

The survey crew stopped at each of the Spanish Forts as they descended the Mississippi River. After facing many dangers, sheer exhaustion, and near starvation, on June 31, 1797, the men, finally, reached Natchez, their chosen location, to meet with the Spaniards. Ellicott and Gillespie left their military escort at Bayou Pierre as requested by Gayoso, the Spanish Governor of the Natchez Region. With great relief, Ellicott's exhausted expedition crew prepared the American campsite within sight of Fort Panmure.

After a polite reception by Lt. Governor Gayoso,

Ellicott, with Gillespie serving as secretary, met privately with Governor Gayoso. Ellicott discussed with the Spaniards the principle purpose of their American mission. Ellicott clearly explained to Gayoso that America's mission was to establish the Florida line, the 31st parallel of latitude. America desired the cooperation of the Governor as Spain's assigned treaty commissioner.

The Spanish Louisiana Governor Baron de Carondelet, meanwhile, tried everything possible to delay the Florida survey, and otherwise undermine terms of the treaty. He dispatched his emissary to Kentucky, and the North West territory with large amounts of money, through America's General Wilkinson. The Spanish Governor created dissatisfaction and encouraged a separation from America. Even though King Charles IV of Spain suspended Mississippi trade restrictions, after signing the Madrid (Pinckney-Goday) Treaty, Spain had no intentions to surrender the Louisiana territory as agreed. Under pressure from Britain and France, and the United States, Charles signed the Treaty. Earlier, Britain planned an invasion of Louisiana; fortunately, the British suspended their invasion after Spain signed the Madrid Treaty.

With Spain's attempt to delay the survey, the local Natchez populous, the Spaniards in the Fort, and Ellicott's survey crew became very restless and tense. Open hostilities between the American survey party and the Spaniards appeared inevitable.

A high state of military readiness continued throughout all that spring and summer. To further irritate the Ellicott and Gillespie survey party, the Spaniards paid the Indians to perform a tribal war dance through Natchez with brilliantly decorated tomahawks. The many brightly painted warriors wore colorful head plumes and made thunderous, ear piercing war whoops, and merrily danced throughout the American campsite.

Gillespie and party sat quietly in their tents and

prayed for safety. Finally the warriors became tired of whooping and dancing and faded into the darkness. During this period, Ellicott, the Spaniards, the local Natchez folks, and the Indians argued continuously.

On May, 6 1798, the Spanish Governor General gave official word that Spain was surrendering the territory. Upon receiving approval from Spain to begin the survey, Ellicott immediately pulled out of Natchez. Many in Natchez were elated to see Ellicott leave town.

Soon after beginning the Boundary Survey, six miles below Fort Adams at the Bayou Tunica, Ellicott and Thomas Freeman's many disagreements resulted in a violent argument. Meanwhile, General Wilkinson was in the surveying camp. Immediately, Wilkinson fired Freeman from the survey. Supposedly, Wilkinson visited the surveying camp to check the progress of the survey. Suspicions were that Wilkinson wanted to demonstrate to the Spaniards that he was the number one American in charge of the Florida- Mississippi Territory. Recognizing David's enormous surveying talents, Ellicott assigned David the full responsibility for conducting the Florida survey.

David was well prepared and trained for his new assignment as America's surveyor. In David's early teen years, his father extensively taught him surveying. His father taught David how to survey with the transit and the equal altitude instrument in conjunction with a telescope and surveyor compass. David received excellent preparatory instruction at the Grove Preparatory Academy and intensive mathematic and Astronomy teaching from Professor Harris at UNC.

David now had responsibility for all secretarial duties of the meetings with Spanish Governmental officials as well as responsibilities for recording detailed astronomical observations and calculations for the survey to mark precisely the Florida line, the 31st Parallel.

Ellicott's astronomical equipment for determining longitude and latitude surpassed other survey instruments of the period. Ellicott carefully set his observatory tent, with a hole in top to observe the horizon, from the highest point available. He used a minimum of two zenith sectors for tracing a meridian to lay off an angle for his triangulation calculations. Key to his astronomical observations and calculations was his unique very accurate astronomical clock to ensure precise timing of the star trajectories measured in the night's horizon.

Supported by Ellicott's astronomical measurements made from his observatory tent, David Gillespie surveyed the Florida line using Ellicott's handmade transit and equal altitude instrument in conjunction with a zenith telescope to pin point the north star within a degree or two of the zenith for determining his exact location on the earth's surface. David used the surveyor's compass to assist in determining directional lines in accordance with the true meridian. The compass with a variation arc, and vernier mechanism, provided fine adjustments to offset for magnetic north; thus, allowing lines of survey to be run to the true meridian (true north).

Ellicott patterned his hand made survey instruments after London's John Bird's transit-altitude instruments, earlier purchased by William Penn for the Mason and Dixon survey to establish the colonial boundaries between Maryland and Pennsylvania.

On 21st May 1798, the American surveying crew led by Ellicott and Gillespie joined with Stephen Minor, Commissioner for Spain, and a party of woodsmen to cut and mark the line. On the 26th, William Dunbar, Spain's Astronomical Commissioner, joined the surveying effort. Dunbar's engineering and surveying talents were widely acclaimed. His Natchez plantation, "The Forest," served as a frequent meeting place for scholars of the day, including William Bartram the naturalist, and Alexander Wilson the ornithologist.

Ellicott began hiring additional men to help with the survey and Dunbar suggested that he hire a local Natchez young lad John Walker. He was the son of Peter Walker, servant to Gayoso. Walker became third in line working on the survey. John Walker soon won Gillespie's respect and friendship with his responsive day-to-day assistance. David especially liked Walker's quick wit and sense of humor and enthusiastically taught him how to survey.

Stephen Minor, Spain's Provisional field manager for the survey, supervised the supply of all Spanish provisions. Minor brought his own cook who provided superb dinners for the Spanish survey crew. Occasionally, David and John Walker, through Walker's influence, shared the many delicacies of the Spanish.

The Spaniards efficiently managed their survey crew. The Spanish provided their survey party with the finest survey instruments, plenty of food, and excellent pay. Ellicott's operations lacked effective leadership. They were short on food and paid much less than the Spaniards.

To run the Florida survey, David Gillespie walked many days on end through dangerous swamps; endured swarms of mosquitoes, many other biting insects, and deadly rattlesnakes.

The survey crew cut a wide path through thick bamboo forests which were especially difficult to penetrate. Gillespie and his survey crew marked the line approximately every mile with a mound of earth about five feet high. The crew vertically centered each mound with a large pole accurately marking the 31st parallel as the Florida line. Today some of these mounds, formed by Gillespie, are found across the swamps, farms and byways of the 31st parallel. The location of these mounds are of much historic interest to today's surveyors.

Nearly every night Ellicott and his son indulged in sex with a Spanish mistress whose sexual favors they enjoyed throughout the entire 1½-year survey across the Florida wilderness. Everyone in camp, especially Gillespie, Stephen Minor and Peter Walker, were shamefully aware of Ellicott and his son, Andy's, ménage a trios with their Spanish harlot.

David was highly religious, much embarrassed, and extremely troubled by Ellicott's sexual misconduct, lack of leadership, and arrogant behavior. He wrote to his father, Congressman Gillespie, in Philadelphia a number of letters describing his dissatisfaction and his concern over such small payment for such an important undertaking.

David through his close day-to-day contact and interface for many days with the Spanish surveying crew, and particularly with horse trader Philip Nolan, learned of General Wilkinson's treasonous activities with the Spaniards. He learned that Wilkinson accepted huge bribes paid in gold from the Spanish to encourage settlers in the Louisiana and Kentucky territory to support Spain. Earlier, Philip Nolan, for a number of months, worked directly for Wilkinson as his aide and secretary with full knowledge of Wilkinson's activities of treason with the Spaniards.

David cautiously reported his information about Wilkerson accepting Spanish bribes to Ellicott. David hesitated to inform his father Congressman Gillespie of his discovery of Wilkinson's treason. He was worried that the Spanish would intercept his letter describing Wilkinson's alleged treason.

Ellicott and Gillespie gathered more information about Wilkinson's activities as time elapsed. Several weeks later, they intercepted an encrypted note from General Gayoso to inn a cask of sugar. Using a Spanish pocket dictionary Ellicott and Gillespie translated the letter. The letter implicated Wilkinson, Senator John Brown, a judge Sebastian and other opportunists Mr. Murray and Lackasang in a conspiracy with Spain to gain control of Kentucky and Tennessee. These five men received bribes from Spain to stir up unrest in the region and to support the Spaniards grandiose scheme of hoping to gain control of the Mississippi Territory.

Ellicott and Gillespie carefully prepared an encrypted letter for Secretary of State Pickering reporting their discovery and details of General Wilkinson's treason. Carefully Ellicott forwarded his secret message to Secretary Pickering with the next American messenger going to Philadelphia.

A few years later during the Aaron Burr Congressional inquiry under President Jefferson, the information discovered by Gillespie and Ellicott was supported in sworn testimony. Senator Brown of Kentucky, Judge Sebastian, and Wilkinson were named for their participation in the Spanish plot. However, under the Constitution, two percipient witnesses were needed to convict Burr of treason.

Philip Nolan who worked briefly for Ellicott was also aware of the Spanish plot. Spanish Governor Manuel Gayoso was not pleased when he saw Nolan with Gillespie and the American surveying party. Nolan was well educated, and earlier worked for Wilkinson as his business secretary and bookkeeper. Nolan obtained, using Wilkinson's influence, a Spanish trading pass for both Louisiana and West Florida.

Nolan was quite the horse trader all across Texas and Louisiana. On his many trips across the Texas Louisiana frontier to capture wild horses he produced a detailed map of the region, which he passed on to Wilkinson. Nolan's luck finally ran out when he crossed the Mexican Spanish border without a Spanish pass. He was hunted down and killed in a shootout with Spanish soldiers in what is today's Nolan River, a branch of the Brazos.

Many friends in high places apparently, supported Wilkinson's operation. In 1803, he shared the honor of taking possession of the Louisiana Purchase and became the First Governor of the Louisiana Territory. Wilkinson very often abused his power. In an attempt to save himself, during Burr's trial, he revealed Aaron Burr's plans to set up an independent nation in the west.

Wilkinson testified at Burr's trial, which led to public accusations against him. In 1811, President Madison ordered his court martial but the court found Wilkinson not guilty. Ironically, President Madison appointed Wilkinerson a Major General in War of 1812. Upon leading two failed campaigns, the Government relieved Wilkinson of his duties. Following his dismissal from the military, a military inquiry cleared him of any wrongdoing. In 1821, he went to Mexico to carry out a Texas land grant scheme and while waiting for Mexican approval of his Texas land scheme he died in Mexico City.

In 1854, Louisiana historian Charles Gayarre, who wrote "The History of Louisiana", provided positive proof that Wilkinson was heavily involved in bribery and land swindle schemes with Spain and Spain's Louisiana Governor. The treason scheme that David Gillespie and Andrew Ellicott uncovered during their Florida survey finally was proven without further doubt.

Midway through the survey, hostile Creek Indians attacked David Gillespie when mistakenly he instructed his survey crew to mark the line over the top of a large Creek burial mound. The Creek warriors attacked Gillespie's surveying crew killing several members of the party. Fortunately, the Creek Chief stopped the massacre before his warriors killed David. The Creek chief earlier had promised Benjamin Hawkins to provide protection for David Gillespie and his party, especially since David's father, Congressman Gillespie, was a close friend of Senator Hawkins.

Secretary of State Pickering's office, for a short time, reported that the Creeks killed David Gillespie. A few weeks later, United States Senator Timothy Bloodworth, a close friend of the family, happily told the Gillespies that their son was alive. Bloodworth had received this wonderful news through a special letter from Benjamin Hawkins reporting that Congressman Gillespie's son David had survived. The Creeks had killed several members of the surveying party.

David's letter to brother Joseph informed him of the bloody Creek warrior attack and his ghastly tasks disposing of slaughtered members of his surveying crew. David's letter described the deadly Creek ambush, and his severe difficulty in notifying family members of those killed. David described the gruesome task of sending home to family members personal effects including a golden pocket watch. Joseph's earlier letter to David referenced problems on their Marsh Creek Plantation; in reply, David indicated he had little time for sympathy under his circumstances.

After David Gillespie and survey crew ran a compass line from the Pearl River near Natchez, Ellicott had a monument stone set overlooking the Mobile River. Today, this stone sits on a height called "Seymour's Bluff" fifty feet above the Mobile River. Ellicott and Gillespie made precise astronomical observations using the stars, the moon, and sun for their triangulation calculations to determine the exact global position for his survey cornerstone. Over the years the United States Public Land survey has used Ellicott's "Seymour's Bluff" as an exact reference for their surveying baseline point. Today, this baseline point is known as St. Stephens Meridian and St. Stephens Baseline. (North side is marked: "U.S. lat. 31"; South side is marked "Dominion of King Charles IV. lat 31-1799.")

- ELLICOTT'S STONE -

     Following continued threats of attack by Creek and Seminole Indians on defenseless David and his survey party, Ellicott decided to terminate the Florida survey at the mouth of the Flint River. He instructed David, in August of 1799, to lead the survey party across hundreds of miles of dangerous Florida Indian occupied swamps over to the St Mary's on the east Coast of Florida.

     Ellicott, meanwhile, took a twenty-ton schooner, the Sally, with instruments, supplies and military escort to set sail around Pensacola and through Key Largo to later join Gillespie at St Mary's on the east coast. As Ellicott sailed by St Marks, he encountered William Bowles and his wife, a Creek Chief's daughter, returning to Pensacola to rule the region. Bowles with his Creek Indian tribe soon captured the Fort at St Marks located on the confluence of the

Appalachia River.

At age fifteen, Warren Augustine Bowles became an officer in the British Royal Navy. The British discharged Bowles for dereliction of duty when he missed his British Navy Ship in Pensacola. Bowles ran from the British into North Florida to the safety and support of the Creek Indians. Bowles married the Muskogee chief's daughter. When the Muskogee Chief died, Bowles inherited the Muskogee Kingdom. In 1787 at age 17, Bowles led a Muskogee battle against Spain that lost his Pensacola territory to Spain. Bowles escaped to the Bahamas. British General Lord Dunmore sent Bowles back to the Muskogee nation to establish British trade. Britain's King George III supported Bowles in his idea to establish a combined Creek -Cherokee Nation. With British support, Bowles trained the Creeks as pirates to attack Spanish ships.

In 1795, Bowles along with the Seminoles formed a short-lived state in North Florida known as Muskogee. In 1799, the Muskogee Indian nation appointed Bowles as head of their state. During the years of Ellicott's survey, Bowles as leader of the Muskogees occupied land claimed by both Spain and the United States. The ambitious Bowles had aspirations of establishing a large state of Muskogee in Florida, Alabama, Georgia, North Carolina and Tennessee. In 1803, Bowles was leader of the Creeks and known as the Chief of all Indians in the Mississippi territory. Soon, the Muskogees betrayed Bowles and allowed his capture by Spain. The Spaniards imprisoned Bowles in Havana Cuba where he died.

Ellicott sailed along the Gulf shore through the Straits of Key Largo into the Atlantic Ocean. In sailing up the Atlantic he was chased by pirates who finally gave up their pursuit.

On December 8, 1799, Ellicott arrived at St Mary's and found David and his survey crew resting under a large palm tree. Unlike Ellicott's sailing adventure, David and his survey party endured a three hundred mile journey across the dangerous Florida wilderness swamps. Due to torrential rains during his long trek from the Flint River, David and his survey crew's long journey was unusually difficult. Unable to find suitable quarters in St Mary's, Ellicott and Gillespie camped their surveying party under a grove of oaks at St. Point Peter on the Georgia line.

On the 19th of January in 1800, Ellicott and Gillespie completed the Florida line observations at Point Peter, and rowed up to the end of St Mary's River with several laborers of the survey. They then canoed the remaining water up to the edge of the Okefenokee Swamp. Gillespie and Captain Minor at the swamp's edge instructed the laborers to build a mound which today marks where Georgia and Florida land ended and the St. Mary's River begins. On 27th February 1800, Ellicott completed his Commission for the Madrid Treaty that astronomically established the Florida Boundary. The Ellicott mound, which terminated Ellicott's Florida survey, is located on official Georgia-Florida Maps.

Ellicott and Gillespie, with their crew, boated back to Cumberland Island. The next day Ellicott and his survey party set sail with their schooner Sally up to the Savannah River, arriving on April 5, 1800. At this point, Ellicott relinquished the Schooner Sally to the government to be used on local Savannah Rivers.

Gillespie, Ellicott, Andy Ellicott, John Walker and other respective crewmembers chartered a sloop for Philadelphia that arrived at the Market Street Wharf on May 18, 1800. Standing on the wharf, many cheering Philadelphia spectators paid especial attention to Congressman Gillespie's young son, David, presumed murdered by Creek warriors. The survey instruments used by Gillespie and mostly hand made by Ellicott are today enshrined in the Smithsonian Institute.

Ellicott's and David Gillespie's survey established a

boundary between the U. S. and South-West Spanish territories and was the young nation's first diplomatic victory, the first acquisition of territory outside the thirteen colonies and the beginning of the manifest destiny for America's national expansion in prevailing over the colonization of England , France and Spain.

On June 15, 1800, David Gillespie returned home to the Village of Grove, a hero for America. David's brave, tireless efforts provided America shipping rights on the Mississippi River and ensured settlement of territorial disputes with Spain. With David's return to the "Village of Grove", there was much jubilation by David's many Scots-Irish friends at Sheriff Pearsall's tavern which lasted until early the next morning.

David was away from home for three and one half years. He had not seen his mother Dorcus, other family members, or friends during his long and dangerous trek across the Florida swamps. David was much alarmed over his mother's health. During his absence, his mother became very frail and bedridden most of the time. David was home at their plantation only five and one half months when his mother died on November 29, 1800 at age 50. The Gillespie family buried their beloved wife and mother, Dorcus at the nearby Grove Presbyterian Cemetery known today as the Routledge Cemetery.

Successful completion of the Florida survey required not only keen surveying skills but also successful diplomacy with the Spaniards and the inhabitants of Natchez to gain their cooperation. Even though Ellicott received numerous compliments from President Adams and Secretary of State Pickering, Adams refused to release Ellicott's Notes and records preventing Ellicott from writing his Journal. Ellicott had difficulty in receiving full compensation for his significant scientific accomplishments and one of the young nation's greatest diplomatic achievements with Spain. Finally, through the encouragement of Thomas Jefferson and several congressional representatives, including James Gillespie, President Adams finally released Ellicott's records and notes. Hesitantly, he to some degree compensated Ellicott and David Gillespie for their extensive, difficult, and extremely dangerous expedition.

Jefferson Survey Commissions Following the Florida Survey

After the Florida survey and following the Louisiana Purchase, Jefferson commissioned surveyor Dunbar in 1804 to lead the Red River Expedition that became known as the Grand Expedition. This expedition to explore the Red, Black, and Quachuto River Basins of the Louisiana Purchase ended abruptly, due to conflicts with the Spaniards and Osage Indians. Dunbar brought back information on the Hot Springs of Arkansas.

Jefferson sanctioned four explorations of the Louisiana Territory: Lewis and Clark's, Dunbar's, Thomas Freeman's (the surveyor General Wilkinson fired) and Zebulon Pike's. Freeman explored the Red River in 1806. Following the Florida survey, Freeman and David Gillespie continued their friendship through letters that today are in the Library of Congress contained among the Ellicott papers.

John Walker, trained by David Gillespie on the Florida line as a surveyor, left Natchez in 1800 for Philadelphia where Ellicott hired him to draw maps of the United States-Spanish Boundary. Walker made an impressive six-foot high tin map of Gillespie and Ellicott's boundary survey. When the British burned Washington in the War of 1812 they destroyed this large tin art masterpiece by Walker. Zebulon Pike selected Walker to assist him in his exploration of the southwest. In 1811, Spain jailed Walker for his support of the Mexican Independence movement and banished him to a Spanish prison.

In 1803, Ellicott wrote to Thomas Jefferson responding to the President's request for surveying assistance for Meriwether Lewis. Ellicott responded, "Mr. President, I would be very pleased and happy to train Meriwether Lewis on how to record astronomical measurements on his trip westward." He informed President Jefferson that all the information and instruction in his power was available for the Lewis and Clark expedition, the nation's most interesting and significant North West expedition. Ellicott spent a number of days with Lewis and diligently instructed him how to obtain distance and direction with his surveying instruments. One of Ellicott's main instruments for instruction included his gridiron pendulum adapted in a regulator. Ellicott also recommended an Arnold chronometer along with a special stopwatch as two key recording devices. Ellicott stressed to Lewis the importance of recording measurements carefully and accurately. He also instructed Lewis due to the burden of recording numerous calculations for triangulation that he should make his many calculations after his return home.

Ellicott, after reviewing Gillespie's many astronomical calculations and finding them to be extremely accurate, finalized his Florida Survey Document. He submitted his Florida Survey report to President Adams. Adams reluctantly accepted Ellicott's report without compensating Ellicott for his numerous charts and detailed surveys. Ellicott desired to publish his report; however, President Adams refused Ellicott's access to his survey report which delayed his Journal being published. In 1803, with Jefferson as President and with huge encouragement from Congressman James Gillespie, the Federal Government finally returned to Ellicott his report. Ellicott immediately made final arrangements for publishing his Florida Survey Journal which was instrumental in gaining control of the Mississippi River.

In 1803, Governor McKean of Pennsylvania

appointed Ellicott Secretary of the Pennsylvania Land office. Ellicott moved to Lancaster, Pennsylvania to manage the land office. In 1808 when General Wilkinson's friend Snyder became Governor of Pennsylvania, Ellicott lost his job as Pennsylvania Land Office Secretary. In the winter of 1810 to 1811, Ellicott testified in Washington D. C. at the Wilkinson trial. In 1810 Ellicott abandoned his plans to build an observatory sponsored by the Philosophical Society for the University of Pennsylvania. His lifelong dream of building an observatory was destroyed by Governor Snyder who spitefully sold the intended site owned by the State. Snyder, a friend of General Wilkerson, retaliated against Ellicott for his continual insistence that Wilkerson was involved in a treasonous plot with the Spaniards relative to the Louisiana territory.

Following the return of the Lewis and Clark expedition in 1807, Thomas Jefferson signed an act to establish an agency for surveying America's coast. The Agency, "The United States Coast Survey", originally under the Army was to identify all islands, shoals, and the best sites for anchorage. One of Jefferson's objectives for the agency was to stimulate International trade.

Jefferson consulted the Philosophical Society in which he, Ellicott, and other leading scientists were members, to identify qualified surveyors. Benjamin Franklin started the society, which is similar to today's Academy of Sciences. Among the many proposals received were Ellicott's, James Madison's, and a Swiss geophysicist by the name of Hassler. Jefferson recognizing the outstanding reputation and experience of Hassler selected him to manage the coastal survey.

Hassler selected David Gillespie, due to his expertise in triangulation, as his assistant for the Coastal survey. Earlier, Hassler received a letter of recommendation for David from Ellicott confirming David

Gillespie's expertise in surveying using triangulation. Jefferson in discussions with Hassler confirmed the surveying abilities of David Gillespie.

Part IX - The Death of a True Defender of the Rights for Common Man (1805)
Chapter 27
Congressman James Gillespie's Congressional Funeral

James Gillespie endured the many long years of hardship in the United States Congress away from his Duplin plantation and his family. In 1798, he fell on the icy streets of Philadelphia and broke his hip. From this point in time James' health began to fail. James died in Washington D.C. on January 11, 1805 at the end of his 4th term in the United States Congress.

His congressional funeral was held at the "Old Bridge" Street Presbyterian Church in Georgetown. Reverend Stephen Balch, minister of the Old Bridge Church, presided over the funeral service. During this period, with the location of the Capital in Washington, a number of Presbyterian Congressman, including James Gillespie, supported remodeling the small and quaint Old Bridge Presbyterian church of Georgetown.

Since there were few churches in the nation's new capital, many members of Congress, in the late 1700's and early 1800's, attended church in the Capital. They used the house chambers as their sanctuary. Many congressional members were staunch Presbyterians and attended Georgetown's Old Bridge, Presbyterian Church. Like Gillespie, a number of Congressmen during sessions of Congress resided in Georgetown and frequented Georgetown's "Old Tavern", which today serves as a club.

Thomas Jefferson, who James so greatly honored, was unable to attend Congressman Gillespie's funeral. He sent his words of kindness and praise to the Gillespie family with sincere appreciation for James Gillespie's many long years of faithful service to his Presidency. Jefferson words of praise were, "James Gillespie's heroic war efforts and his distinguished congressional service, fighting for the rights of the "common man" are so greatly appreciated by America. James had expressed many times during our legislative sessions how proud he was to be an Anti-Federalist. He, like I, proudly supported the adoption of a "Bill of Rights" in the Constitution, and very much supported religious freedom and many times expressed sincere appreciation for my Virginia statute for religious freedom."

Members of Congress who attended James' funeral to memorialize his Anti-Federalist's efforts included his colleagues Macon, Martin and Bloodworth. As Anti-Federalists, these colleagues of James steadfastly supported the rights for "common man" and Jefferson's Presidency. His two sons, David and Joseph, were among the family members who attended Congressman Gillespie's memorial service. David gave the funeral's eulogy.

David's eulogy message was, "Our father James is laid to rest knowing our nation's citizens are truly **FREE.** His courageous, heroic, efforts in our war for Independence and his diplomatic genius in Congress have ensured that our new nation has **FREEDOM.**

Our father's great-grandfather, George Gillespie, his brother Patrick, the other great Covenanter Presbyterian evangelist, and the many Scots-Irish who suffered so much over many years at the hands of cruel English Kings would be so very proud of our new nation. Our Scottish forefathers would be so pleased and joyous over America's 'Freedom' that was won with the enormous support of the brave Scots-Irish Presbyterians who fought so heroically in the battles of Carolina's backwoods. The severe sacrifices of our brave Scots-Irish forefathers will always be remembered and cherished."

"In closing, our father was most proud of his political efforts in insisting that America's Constitution included a 'Bill of Rights' to ensure individual

FREEDOM, especially "**FREEDOM OF RELIGION**." "Please let President Jefferson know how thankful our father was and our family is, for the President's Virginia Statute for religious freedom which ensured that no man shall be compelled to support, attend any religious worship against their will, or be persecuted for their religious worship as our forefathers were over centuries by the English Crown."

In 1805, Congressman Gillespie was laid to rest in a small burial plot next to the Old Bridge Presbyterian Church on Bridge Street. In 1821,Gillespie's grave was moved to a new Georgetown Presbyterian church burial ground between 34th & Q Streets and Volta place, a short distance from Georgetown's, earlier, small Presbyterian church. Over much of the 1800's the continual growth of Georgetown caused much uproar between the "Presbyterian Committee of Church Property" and Georgetown residents over the location of the Presbyterian Church Cemetery in downtown Georgetown. Finally in 1892, Gillespie's body was moved to the Congressional Cemetery behind the capital, along Anacostia River.

"North Carolina Congressman Gillespie's Grave at Congressional Cemetery" –Photo by Mike Peele

FREEDOM TIDES

Surely the High Tide of Freedom had arrived for the Scots-Irish clan of Gillespies, Pearsalls, Rutledges, Dicksons, and Stallings from Duplin, N. C.'s "Village of Grove" and all the other Scots-Irish Presbyterians across America's countryside who turned the tide in the war to victory over the British and their cruel Kings (Stuarts) and their beastly Generals (Tarleton). From the Crown's horrific drownings at the seashore by the rising tides, to the high tide of victory at Yorktown, the Scots- Irish Presbyterians finally gained their **FREEDOM**.

"Let freedom ring. Let everyone feel its inspiration."

EPILOGUE

The brave Scots-Irish Presbyterian's suffered so dreadfully in their steadfast crusade for **FREEDOM** from the Crown's cruelties; especially cruelties of the Stuart Kings, which were summarily justified through their Kingly Rights. Over centuries, the Covenanters continually fought the English crown to ensure the British Isles obtained liberties and Freedom of Religion for the common man through England and Scotland's "Bill Of Rights". These freedom-loving Scots-Irishmen emigrated to America with an intense burning flame for liberty, ensuring the new nation of America won its Freedom from the unjust rule of the English Crown and continual absurdities of Kingly Rights.

Scots-Irish immigrants like James Gillespie of Duplin and the Gillespie brothers, Daniel and John, of Mecklenburg, refused to ratify the Constitution. Long remembering England's unjust Kingly Rights, they and colleagues held out insisting on better controls over the Federal Government. Sadly, their significant efforts did not gain the Federal Government controls they so much desired and had the wisdom and farsight to envision as necessary to protect the rights of the common man. The political power of the Federalists, with their rich merchant support driven by President Adams, and to some degree by Washington, was too strong to allow inclusion of necessary controls in the Constitution.

These early American pioneers of democracy were such great visionaries with their vehement fight for definitive controls, controls so critically needed today. Sadly, the Anti-Federalist's vision for more definitive Congressional controls is critically needed in the 21st century to control today's selfish political maneuvers of Congress.

SOURCES

I- Images
1. Wikipedia Common Images. The following images used in this "Quest for Freedom" story are in the **Public Domain** and are not restricted under any copyright: Wallace Statue image, Solemn League Covenant, Kirkcaldy Kirk (Attribution "User Kilburn"), Westminster Assembly, Glasgow University Memorial Gates, Cromwell Tower-King College Aberdeen, Tryon Palace, Thomas Jefferson's tombstone Monticello, Charles Wemar's rescue of Henderson & Boone, Ellicott's Stone and Signing of Covenant at Greyfriars, Fayetteville's Cool Spring Tavern, Geneva Bible. Chronicle of England, Bruce kills Henry De Bohun.

2. **Creative Commons Images used** – Free Use Provisions. As specified under Creative Commons' website (Creativecommons.org) the following images are incorporated as per their free use provisions. These images can only be shared and remixed as specified under Creative Commons' attribution and share alike conditions. Much appreciation is extended to **Creative Commons** for free use of these images. Holy Rude Kirk, St. Giles Cathedral, Bass Rock, Derry Walls Castle Gates, James Gillespie's Tombstone by Mike Peele.

2- B Education Scotland – Open Government Licence- **Scotland's National Covenant**

3. Dr. David Gillespie's House (vines on side porch) – Courtesy of N.C. State Archives

II- Written Material
Both primary and secondary resource material were used in writing this book. The primary material came from discussions over the years with State Archives and University history researchers. In particular much was learned through Dr. Schrader, former Director of UNC's Southern Historical Library, about the founding of the

University of North Carolina in which the McCorkle-Gillespie families were intimately involved. Scotland's University of Glasgow provided much valuable information about Patrick Gillespie, former Principal of the University, and his association with Oliver Cromwell under the Gillespie Charter, which greatly supported Scotland's Universities.

The many secondary sources include a wide range of websites, in particular Wikipedia, books, as well as a number of movies (e.g. Braveheart, Elizabeth, Rob Roy and The Patriot). Among the sources analyzed for content to support the Presbyterian's "Quest for Freedom" was:

Part I- Scotland's Yearning for Freedom (1296-1603)

-Movie Brave Heart- The portrayal of William Wallace's bravery, his hideous hanging, and de-bowling forms this chapter's nucleus.

-History of Scotland- & Kingdom of Scotland-by Barrow

-Edinburgh's University Press has a fine overview of the fierce determined born- fighting spirit of the Scottish warriors

-The National Archives of Scotland are recommended for review of Scotland's Declaration of Aberoth

-Details of History of Roman Catholicism is provided by--Encyclopedia Britannica

-Jack Zavada's, John Knox, biography is a valuable resource for reviewing John Knox's life and his leadership during the protestant Reformation

-King Henry's Rough Wooing- Lancaster University's Scottish historian Marcus Merriman's "The Rough Wooings" provides unique insight relative to King Henry's atrocities.

-Bloody Queen Mary- Readers are directed to the Luminary Encyclopedia

-Fox's Book of Martyrs - Records Bloody Mary's

hideous burning of more than 280 helpless Puritans.
-Whittingham and the Geneva Bible: Bruce
Metzger's "The Geneva Bible of 1560" provides an
overview for the translation of the Geneva Bible.
Detailed is the Puritan's translation of the Bible into
English and Whittingham's writing of the New
Testament"
-Movie Queen Elizabeth - Is the focal point & core
of this chapter. The movie provides unique insight
of Catholic- Protestant battles for religious
supremacy. Portrayed are the many Catholic
Schemes to dethrone the Puritan Queen, her
awesome decision to behead Mary of Guise, the
miraculous defeat of King Phillip's mighty Spanish
Armada, and the salvation of her Protestant empire.

**PART II- King James and His Anglican Church – His
"Kingly Rights"- The Presbyterian Covenanter
Revolution-The Stuarts "Killing Fields" (1567-1688)**
-Family records and information from Scotland's
national archives provide much insight as to the
fascinating stories about the Simson-Gillespie
family and their faithful support of Presbyterianism
and their battles against the dictatorial Stuart Kings
-Antonia Fraser's book "King James VI of Scotland
and I of England" provides everything about James
from his birth to death especially his associates and
his life events.
-Patrick Simson- Acts and proceedings of the
"General Assemblies of the Kirk of Scotland"-
Assembly Proceedings provide much insight into
the life of Minister Simson and his trials and
tribulations dealing with King James.
-Ancestory.com provides Simson family info and
discusses Minster Simson and his influence with
King James and the "Countess of Mar". -Robert
Anderson's "Andrew Melville: Lion of Scotland"

portrays the personality and religious principles of Melville in his philosophical dealings (both fiery and kind) with King James. -Writing of the King James Bible -Adam Nicolson's masterfully written book "God's Secretaries" describes the writing of the King James Bible as the greatest writing of English prose ever known; thus, the King James Bible became, throughout the world, the most revered source of Biblical scripture. -Charles I and the Presbyterian Revolution

-Wilson's book "Europe's Tragedy - History of Thirty Years War" has a fine overview of Charles I and his trials and tribulations with Parliament and the Covenanters. Gardnier's "Charles I King of Great Britain and Ireland" offers historical facts.

Hibbert and Stackey's- "Life of Religion War and Treason"- Good discussion about Charles and his beheading by Cornwallis.

-"Project Gutenberg e-book Works" good summary of information from the public domain of Gillespie- provides supplemental information to Author's "Gillespie" family records- Summarizes George Gillespie's huge role in the Westminster Assembly. "Encyclopedia Britannica", Cambridge University Press has a fine overview of Author's famous ancestor George Gillespie

John Coffey's Book - Politics Religion and the British Revolutions provides insight as to the brilliance of Samuel Rutherford's mind. - Cromwell's Parliamentary Rule

-LibertyFund.com provides 45 pages of valuable Cromwellian Parliamentary rule information. Discussed is how James Sharp wormed his way into the Presbyterian Kirk of London and so cleverly sold out Presbyterianism upon the re-crowning of Charles II. He gained for himself an Archbishop position at St Andrews. Details of Patrick Gillespie and his Charter are reviewed.

David Smith's book "Oliver Cromwell Politics and Religion in the English Revolution 1640-1658" provides James' Murderous "Killing Fields" insight as to what drove Cromwell as a soldier, politician, statesman and religious visionary. Discussed is how Cromwell viewed his crusade and how his Protectorate was viewed by others.

"Charles II and his Kingdom 1660- 1685" by Tim Harris traces the political violence in Britain throughout King Charles' reign. Maurice Grant's book "Lion of the Covenanters" describes the persecution of Richard Cameron- Walter Scott's book "Old Mortality" describes the Covenanters persecution, so humbly, through an elderly, dying Covenanter.

PART III- King William's Glorious Revolution and Queen Anne's Reign (1688-1714)

-The Glorious Revolution-- Reference "Battle of Boyne" by Enda O'Boyle & "Londonderry Siege" by George Walker- " English Bill of Rights" by Charles Rivers Editors. These writings provide insight relative to the Glorious Revolution and England's resulting "Bill of Rights

-Queen Anne's Reign and the Union of Parliaments-Edward Gregg's "Bibliography of Queen Anne" provides a good summary of the Queen's "Test Acts" and her Act of Union.

PART IV- "The Jacobite Rebellions" (1689-1745)

-"Jacobite Rebellions" by Michael Barthrop describes details of the rebellions of Jacobites

PART V- America's Presbyterian Rebellion (1750-1781)

-James H. Smylie provides an excellent account summary of the Presbyterian's huge role in the Revolutionary War in his writing "Presbyterians and the American Revolution-an Interpretive Account" -John Fiske's, "The War of Independence" Provides much insight as to America's fight for Independence. Marjorie Kars book -"Breaking Loose Together" describes the pitiful plight of Alamance County's Scots-Irish farmers in dealing with the land swindles of the McCulloch's and the corruptions of Governor Tryon. Rodenboughs "Biography of Alexander Martin" sets forth the important role Governor Martin played in North Carolina's legislative history and that Martin's role was essential to N. C. ratifying America's Constitution.

-Robert Dunkerly's two books: "Battle of Kings' Mountain Eye Witness Account" and "Redcoats on the River" serves to provide much insight as to the Whigs victory over Ferguson and the Loyalist at Kings Mountain. Dunkerly's book: "Redcoats on the River" is an excellent description of the battles in South- Eastern N. C. - Moore's Creek, and the Tory Hole battle of Elizabethtown etc.

PART VI- Founding of a New Nation– Presbyterian Contributions (1781-1795)

-"The Bill of Rights: With Writings that Formed Its Foundation" - Little Books of Wisdom by: James Madison and George Mason

Part VII- Presbyterian Contribution to Higher Education in America (1636-1795)

-Minister Foote's "Sketches of N. C. describes the huge role Presbyterian ministers had in ensuring N.C. colonials received an education. Kemp P. Battles "History of the University of North Carolina" from 1789- 1868 to some degree provides the early history of America's first public University.

Gillespie family records provide detailed insight

from a Gillespie family perspective as to the history of the early beginning of U.N.C.

Part VIII- Settlement of Territorial Disputes with Spain (1796-1800)

-Ellicott's Journal provides an excellent account of the Florida Survey - The survey's dangers and many difficulties endured by Ellicott and David Gillespie, the secretary and surveyor for the four year expedition, were accurately recorded for America's prosperity. (The many family letters and records of the Gillespie family provide much insight from a Gillespie family perspective as to the actual day to day difficulties and dangers experienced by David Gillespie during this survey that were vital to founding America.)

PART IX- A True Defender of the Rights of Common Man (1805)

-Reference The Presbyterian Congregation in Georgetown (1780-1970) –Published by the Session of the Presbyterian Congregation in Georgetown provides a brief history of the Presbyterian Church in Georgetown and its trials and tribulations with the Georgetown citizens relative to the existence of the Church's graveyard. My ancestor Congressman George Gillespie's grave was moved several times. Finally, his grave rests at its existing location in the Congressional Cemetery East of the Capital. (Gillespie Family records provide insight as to Congressman Gillespie's funeral.)

THE AUTHORS

David B. Nolan practices constitutional law before the U. S. Supreme Court and is a litigator in complex civil and criminal matters. He is a former White House attorney in the Reagan Administration. His professional writing began in 1972 with the conservative weekly, Human Events .

For the U. S. Department of Energy, Headquarters, Washington D. C. Mr. Nolan was the Senior Trial Attorney for the civil and criminal enforcement of Nuclear Safety requirements.

Under the Office of the Secretary, U. S. Department of Treasury Mr. Nolan recommended final agencyl decisions for **EEO** complaints for the agency's 120,000 employees.

Mr. Nolan is the founder of the Federal Ethics Center @www.FederalEthicsCenter.net and Federal Ethics Center.com.

His most recent professional writing is the 2013 play, "**The Trial of Lee Harvey Oswald**." His literary work is the most iconoclastic since Oliver Stone's screenplay for the movie "JFK." Mr. Nolan is available to lecture on a variety of subjects: including Constitutional Law and the assassination of President John F. Kennedy.

Mr. Nolan holds degrees from Duke University, American University, and the University of La Verne. He did post Juris Doctor study at George Town University Law School and the University of Pennsylvania ,Wharton School of Business.

He may be reached at 97 Willow Run Drive, Centreville Ma., 02632 or 571-277-3265.

William E. Moore is a graduate of N.C. State University with a degree in Mechanical Engineering. He attended George Washington University's graduate school of Engineering Administration.

Mr. Moore is a Vietnam War Veteran and a graduate of "Command General Staff College". He served as a senior military officer for 27 years in the U. S. Army Reserves.

In his civilian career he worked as an Engineer Research Scientist developing electrical power system components. During his career he served as a Research director for the Army's Engineer Research and Development Laboratories and the Department of Energy's, Fossil Energy Research Directorate.

Mr. Moore holds patents in the area of electrical power generation and has authored a number of technical publications in his engineering field of expertise.

Mr. Moore can be reached at **mosby44@msn.com** for Gillespie family history and genealogy.